FOUL DEEDS AND SUSPICIOUS DEATHS AROUND UXBRIDGE

TRUE CRIME FROM WHARNCLIFFE
Foul Deeds and Suspicious Deaths Series

Barking, Dagenham & Chadwell Heath
Barnsley
Bath
Bedford
Birmingham
Black Country
Blackburn and Hyndburn
Bolton
Bradford
Brighton
Bristol
Cambridge
Carlisle
Chesterfield
Colchester
Coventry
Croydon
Derby
Dublin
Durham
Ealing
Folkestone and Dover
Grimsby
Guernsey
Guildford
Halifax
Hampstead, Holborn and St Pancras
Huddersfield
Hull

Leeds
Leicester
Lewisham and Deptford
Liverpool
London's East End
London's West End
Manchester
Mansfield
More Foul Deeds Birmingham
More Foul Deeds Chesterfield
More Foul Deeds Wakefield
Newcastle
Newport
Norfolk
Northampton
Nottingham
Oxfordshire
Pontefract and Castleford
Portsmouth
Rotherham
Scunthorpe
Southend-on-Sea
Staffordshire and The Potteries
Stratford and South Warwickshire
Tees
Warwickshire
Wigan
York

OTHER TRUE CRIME BOOKS FROM WHARNCLIFFE

A-Z of Yorkshire Murder
Black Barnsley
Brighton Crime and Vice 1800-2000
Durham Executions
Essex Murders
Executions & Hangings in Newcastle
    and Morpeth
Norfolk Mayhem and Murder

Norwich Murders
Strangeways Hanged
The A-Z of London Murders
Unsolved Murders in Victorian and
    Edwardian London
Unsolved Norfolk Murders
Unsolved Yorkshire Murders
Yorkshire's Murderous Women

Please contact us via any of the methods below for more information or a catalogue.
WHARNCLIFFE BOOKS
47 Church Street – Barnsley – South Yorkshire – S70 2AS
Tel: 01226 734555 – 734222 Fax: 01226 – 734438
E-mail: enquiries@pen-and-sword.co.uk
Website: www.wharncliffebooks.co.uk

Foul Deeds & Suspicious Deaths Around
UXBRIDGE

JONATHAN OATES

Series Editor
Brian Elliott

Wharncliffe Books

First published in Great Britain in 2008 by
Wharncliffe Books
an imprint of
Pen & Sword Books Ltd
47 Church Street
Barnsley
South Yorkshire
S70 2AS

ISBN 978 18456 30 713

A CIP catalogue record for this book is available from the British Library

Typeset in 11/13pt Plantin by
Mac Style, Nafferton, East Yorkshire

Printed and bound in the UK by
CPI

Pen & Sword Books Ltd incorporates the Imprints of Pen & Sword
Aviation, Pen & Sword Maritime, Pen & Sword Military, Wharncliffe Local
History, Pen and Sword Select, Pen and Sword Military Classics and
Leo Cooper.

For a complete list of Pen & Sword titles please contact
PEN & SWORD BOOKS LIMITED
47 Church Street, Barnsley, South Yorkshire, S70 2AS, England
E-mail: enquiries@pen-and-sword.co.uk
Website: www.pen-and-sword.co.uk

Contents

Acknowledgments		**6**
Other Uxbridge Murders		**6**
Introduction		**7**
Chapter 1	Uxbridge and its Environs	**10**
Chapter 2	Law and Order in and around Uxbridge	**19**
Chapter 3	A Turbulent Priest, 1529–1534	**27**
Chapter 4	The Uxbridge Martyrs, 1555	**33**
Chapter 5	Marital Strife in Harefield, 1784	**37**
Chapter 6	A Regency Whodunit in Yiewsley, 1816	**41**
Chapter 7	Horrid and Mysterious Murder near Uxbridge, 1837	**47**
Chapter 8	A Schoolboy Stabbing in Hayes, 1839	**55**
Chapter 9	The Second Stabbing in 1839	**65**
Chapter 10	Murder in Uxbridge, 1869	**69**
Chapter 11	A Family Butcher, 1870	**77**
Chapter 12	The Hayes Tragedy, 1884	**93**
Chapter 13	Who Murdered Sarah Higgs? 1895	**101**
Chapter 14	Murder or Suicide? 1899	**111**
Chapter 15	Dreadful Murder at Yiewsley, 1899	**123**
Chapter 16	The Uxbridge Gas Chamber, 1906	**130**
Chapter 17	Disappearance at Yiewsley, 1934	**135**
Chapter 18	Murder without Motive? 1937	**144**
Chapter 19	The Assailant Who Never Was, 1938	**152**
Chapter 20	Murder by Person or Persons Unknown, 1954	**160**
Chapter 21	Spies in Suburbia, 1961	**169**
Chapter 22	Manslaughter, Murder and Suicide, 1962	**177**
Conclusion		**190**
Bibliography		**191**
Index		**192**

Acknowledgements

I would like to express my gratitude towards a number of people. Philip Sherwood, Eileen Bowlt and Norman Pearce were kind enough to read through my initial typescript and offered many useful suggestions. Philip Sherwood and Reg Eden were very helpful in allowing me to make use of a number of the pictures in their collections. The staff at Uxbridge Library (Hillingdon Heritage Centre) were assiduous in their provision of information and historical sources. Finally I must thank my wife for assisting with the illustrative material.

This book is dedicated to Tony Scott.

Other murders known to have been committed in and around Uxbridge from the sixteenth century to 1962

1509–1547: The bailiff of Colham and his men killed Richard Clynton, an Uxbridge constable.

11 September 1799: James Syme killed William Aldwin in Uxbridge.

2 July 1936: John Ridgley was killed by his mother, Elsie, in Hayes.

14 December 1940: Alfred Nercini killed Kathleen Nercini in Hillingdon.

16 July 1941: Arthur Kellock was killed by George Sainsbury in Hillingdon.

19 December 1941: Leonard Moore was killed by John Jones in Ruislip.

11 July 1945: Ronald Mauri killed Vera Guest in Hillingdon.

16 April 1949: Phyllis Hanson of Ruislip died after an illegal operation.

6 September 1951: Cyril Haggea killed Arthur Grantham in a tea shop in Uxbridge.

9 June 1952: John Godar killed Maureen Cox in Uxbridge.

12 November 1954: Richard Davies was killed by Florence Davies in Hayes.

?20 March 1956: Mary Barnes was killed by Leslie Barnes, who committed suicide in Hayes.

31 December 1958: Joseph Chrimes killed Norah Summerfield in Hillingdon.

Introduction

There are many books about the history of Uxbridge and the surrounding localities, written by esteemed local authors such as Carolynne Cotton, Philip Sherwood, Eileen Bowlt and Ken Pearce, to name but four. Local history usually attempts to tell the story of a town or village and how they changed throughout the centuries, from earliest times to the present day.

This book is also about local history, but unlike similar books, it concentrates on the criminal past. Other books might refer to a particularly famous crime; such as the William Murray murder of 1869 in Carolynne Cotton's *Uxbridge Past*, or that of John Brill in Eileen Bowlt's *Ruislip Past*. The Krogers of Ruislip are not unknown either, partly due to the film and play concerning these spies. The geographical reach of this book is basically the current London borough of Hillingdon, including Hillingdon, Uxbridge, Ruislip, Northwood, Yiewsley, West Drayton and Hayes. On one occasion, I have stepped over the boundary into Buckinghamshire, but there was a crime committed there so terrible that it seemed worthy of inclusion – and it did feature Uxbridge.

Most of the crimes chronicled here have never been explored in detail, and in some cases have never appeared in print since they were first reported in the press (if indeed they ever were). There are few physical signs of these foul deeds left. The memorial in Uxbridge to the martyrs is not one that one would stumble across unaided, and directions are needed to find the grave of the family massacred in Denham in 1870.

It should be noted that this book is not an academic study of the whole gamut of crimes, from theft, to assault, to murder, from the sixteenth century to the present. Such a volume would have its uses, but would neglect the human dimension of the crime and replace it with the statistical. And for most people, crime is about people. Serious crime is one of the most intense human dramas there can be – a fact not overlooked by those writing crime fiction. This book concentrates on twenty instances of serious crime from the early sixteenth century to the sordid 1960s. Most are of murder, but one involves espionage, another martyrs and another a most turbulent priest. We see the drama unfold, meet the characters and discover their motivations, where known. If the case was unsolved, speculation is offered.

Crime fiction is rather different from crime in real life. The former will always tell the reader who was responsible for a crime and why, even if justice is not always done. There are a number of cases here where the killer was never identified. Furthermore, the role of the detective, so important in fictional crime, is often a minimal one – criminals give themselves up or leave so many clues that their capture is easy. Fictional crime once involved country houses and the upper middle class – now one would be forgiven for thinking that middle-class crime is the rule. Nothing could be further from the truth. Real crime usually involves people rather lower down the social scale, as will be seen here. Complex plots and carefully constructed alibis also belong to the fictional world of murder.

Finding the sources for this book was a little like detective work itself, though as always, it was a case of knowing where to look. The Metropolitan Police files at the National Archives and the index to murder and manslaughter from 1891–1963 were useful, as was the electronic catalogue. Yet to use this alone would have meant concentrating almost solely on the 1930s–1960s. This is because, for the earlier cases, there are, unfortunately, no surviving case files. Where they exist, they include witness statements, doctors' reports, police analysis and statements by suspects. So, useful though these were, the field of enquiry had to be broadened. In one case, the available files are still impossible to access, even though they recount a crime of several decades ago.

Newspapers, both national and local, are another a key source of local history. *The Times* on-line is an invaluable source and is available free of charge at many libraries. At a touch of a button, the keyword search allows you to see all the articles which feature that word. So cases between 1785 and 1985 can be located with ease. Local newspapers, such as *The Buckinghamshire Advertiser* and *The Southall-Norwood Gazette*, provided additional information, too. These are also easily available at local libraries, but the accounts they give are often limited. Comparing the witness statements in the newspapers and the actual ones in the police files, one can see that the former are incomplete.

Then, of course, there are the local historians, archivists and librarians. Their knowledge is invaluable in learning of interesting cases and in locating other sources of information. Mr Pearce pointed me in the direction of a number of criminal acts which I would otherwise have overlooked. The staff at Uxbridge Library, especially Gwyn Jones, have also been helpful in providing documents, books and microfilm of newspapers.

Once this information has been gathered together, the writer's task is to put it together in an interesting way, sorting out which facts are more important than others, and avoiding the repetition that is inevitable in newspapers.

The author has written a number of books about real-life crime, as well as several concerning local history. He is not a criminologist, but has lived locally since 2002.

CHAPTER 1

Uxbridge and its Environs

I t is impossible to offer anything resembling a complete history of Uxbridge and its environs in a few pages and the interested reader will note a number of books for further reading in the bibliography. What shall be attempted here is a very brief introduction to a few salient facts about the district's past. The places to be briefly described here are those within the modern borough of Hillingdon, notably Uxbridge, Ruislip, Northwood, West Drayton, Yiewsley, Hayes and Harefield.

For most of its history, the district was rural and by twenty-first-century standards, very sparsely populated. At the time of the Domesday survey in 1086, there were a number of small hamlets here. There was the manor of West Drayton, with a population of about 100. The manor of Ruislip was also in existence. During the Middle Ages, however, Uxbridge became the foremost settlement in the area, though it was part of the manor of Colham and a chapelry of Hillingdon, with St John's as its parish church. This was partly because of its location; being by the river Colne, it was along the main road from London to Oxford, the Oxford Road, later the Uxbridge Road. It also became a market town by virtue of a royal charter, and the centre of manorial administration in the thirteenth century. Flour milling and brewing became Uxbridge's major industries. In Tudor times, West Drayton was the home of courtiers such as William Paget. The Revd Henry Gold of Hayes involved himself in the dangerous game of religious controversy in this period, too, though to tragic effects, as noted in Chapter 3.

In the seventeenth century, national events affected Uxbridge. There were a number of outbreaks of plague; in 1603, 176 people died of it and in 1625, there were another 136 fatalities. But the great plague of 1665 'only' killed 40 inhabitants. Most in these localities seemed to be sympathetic to the Parliamentary cause in the Civil Wars, at least judging by the protestation rolls, where men attested their loyalty. In 1645, the two sides in the Civil War tried to make a peace treaty here, at a house later known as the Treaty House, though without success. In 1688, there was panic in Uxbridge caused by Irish soldiers deserting James II's army as the invading William of Orange advanced towards London. It was feared that these desperate men would attack the town, though happily this was not the case. Uxbridge's local prominence was noted by Daniel Defoe in the early eighteenth century, thus: 'a pleasant large market town, famous in particular, for having abundance of noble seats of gentlemen and persons of quality in the neighbourhood'. John Loveday, an eighteenth-century antiquarian, noted the Crown as Uxbridge's premier inn.

Most in the district were employed in agriculture, until the early twentieth century. But many worked in the brickfields in the eighteenth, nineteenth and early twentieth centuries, too. Giles Hutson recalled that these itinerant workers were rough and troublesome, especially when drunk. In 1861, 175 men in Yiewsley and West Drayton were 'brickies' and 238 worked in farming. By the 1930s, the brickfields were coming to the end

The Frays, Uxbridge, c *1900.* Author's collection

of their existence, but farms persisted throughout this period. The completion of the Grand Junction Canal in 1805 facilitated the brick industry as it meant the finished article could be cheaply and easily sent to London to be used in the building trade; and rubbish, including manure, was sent back, thus fertilizing the cultivated land.

Schooling was limited until the nineteenth century. Private academies flourished, but the church was involved in schooling from the early Victorian era. St Matthew's School in Yiewsley opened in 1872. One of its pupils was Sarah Higgs (see Chapter 13). By 1835, there were five day schools in Uxbridge and five boarding schools. Many schools were single-sex schools, such as Miss Jenning's school for young ladies and the Cave House School, which prepared boys for the professions and universities. Clergymen often ran schools, and the Revd Sturmer taught at one in Hayes in the late 1830s, though with unhappy results as shall be seen in Chapter 8.

Until the late nineteenth century, these villages were very dark at night-time. Yiewsley Vestry did not agree to having gas lights in the High Street and Horton Road until 1897. Some thought that these lights were merely for the convenience of the councillors. Yet street lighting was rarely lit after midnight – to tragic consequences in south Ruislip in 1954 (see Chapter 20).

Although working hours were long, social life played an important part in most people's lives. Indoor entertainments included concerts and theatricals, both by amateurs and by travelling companies. The first cinema came to Yiewsley in 1911. There were also sports clubs; such as the West Drayton Cricket Club, founded in the 1870s. In the nineteenth and early twentieth century, there were hunt meets beginning in West Drayton and Ruislip. Membership of the Uxbridge Yeomanry appealed to those with a taste for playing at soldiers in the nineteenth century.

The villages in the district then were small rural settlements. In 1801, 951 people lived in Harefield, in 1891 the population was still under 2,000. Northwood, which was part of the parish of Ruislip, was smaller still, with 711 souls as late as 1891. Ickenham's and Cowley's populations were only in their

St Martin's Parish Church, Ruislip, c. *1905.* Author's collection

hundreds by the end of the century, too. One reason for the small growth in population was that the villages here were relatively isolated from the outside world. There was a halt on the Great Western Railway at West Drayton from 1838 and a branch line from here to Uxbridge in 1856 (closing in 1962). This made very little difference. Life expectancy was low in any case; in West Drayton it was about 33 in 1866.

Charles Harper, in 1907, made a number of comments about the rural nature of these places, but he also hints about potential changes that the near future might bring. 'Ruislip is a very queer, old-world place, that until quite recently was actually four miles from a railway station'. Of Hayes, he wrote, 'still one of the most rural villages in this remarkably rural county of Middlesex. Hayes is beautiful. The surrounding country is flat, and was until quite recent times an uncultivated waste.' Finally, 'Uxbridge up to now has resolutely refused to be modernised; but now with the terminus of the electric tramway at the extreme end of its High Street and a new railway station just beyond – well, we shall see.'

It was at the turn of the century that developments in transport began to become more significant. The extension of the tramway from Shepherd's Bush as far as Uxbridge in 1904

Ickenham Village, c. 1900. Author's collection

was one of these. The GWR Line (Central Line in 1948) was extended to West Ruislip in 1906 and the Metropolitan Line to Uxbridge in 1904. At first these lines were used by hikers and day trippers coming into the country for their Sunday treat. But it was now also possible to live in the suburbs and work in London, which had not been the case hitherto. The 'Metroland' of Sir John Betjeman now beckoned.

Hayes Railway Station, c. 1950. Philip Sherwood's collection

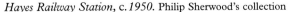

View from Northwood, c. 1900. Author's collection

Local government grew in its powers. Ruislip-Northwood Urban District Council was formed in 1904 from the civil parish of Ruislip. Uxbridge Rural District Council administered Harefield, Ickenham, Hillingdon, Cowley and, until 1928, Northolt. They took over responsibility for public health, town planning and roads, amongst other matters. Apart from Uxbridge (in 1955), however, none ever became an incorporated borough, as some nearby authorities, such as Southall, did.

The First World War had a major effect here, as elsewhere. Charles Mills, MP for Uxbridge, was killed in action in 1915. From Yiewsley, there were 120 fatalities, out of a total of 530 who enlisted. A searchlight unit was established at West Drayton, in case there was any bombing. Railway lines were guarded for fear of saboteurs. Neither of these dangers ever materialized.

Between the World Wars, the population of Uxbridge and its environs, as with the rest of Middlesex, expanded rapidly. But it developed in different ways. Hayes, West Drayton and Yiewsley, being situated by the GWR, and a branch of the Grand Union Canal, became centres of industry. Nestles, Kraft and EMI located in Hayes. Briggs, a contemporary chronicler, described Hayes thus:

Round the station rises the largest group of modern
factories in Middlesex, one firm alone employing some
fifteen thousand hands ... The straggling main road north
and south is a seething mass of cosmopolitan humanity and
becomes almost impassable when the midday and evening
whistles release an army of workers on bicycles.

A booklet produced in 1939 noted that Yiewsley and West
Drayton 'is becoming increasingly prosperous, both from a
residential and commercial standpoint'. There was much that
was unpleasant – the new sludge works erected at Heathrow
by the county council covered 250 acres, and the 'large and
unpleasant refuse-dump' at Yiewsley were hardly amenities.
The latter, though, was a useful place to conceal corpses, as
shall be seen in Chapter 17.

Ruislip and Northwood were described by Briggs,
respectively, as 'a veritable gem among villages' and 'one of the
loveliest villages in the country'. In part this was because over
1,000 acres of woodland and other spaces, including an
artificial lake of 80 acres, had been preserved from being built
upon. These included Mad Bess Wood and Copse Wood.
According to Briggs, writing of Northwood, 'it appears

Mount Vernon Hospital, Northwood, c. 1920. Author's collection

conventional, prosperous, and ordinary, with a strong bias towards golf'. Yet 'the standard of new building in Ruislip is far above the average, thanks to wise direction and artistic taste. Even the modern shops along the High Street are less blatant than usual, and the new post office is charming.'

Uxbridge was still the most important town in the locality, and its transport links were improved in 1938, by the Metropolitan and Piccadilly branches of the Underground railway having their termini here. Markets were still being held here twice weekly. As Briggs wrote in the 1930s:

> The 'quiet village' of Ickenham is now disturbed by a constant thunder of builders' lorries. Opposite the village church you can get a permanent wave or buy gramophone records, or even imbibe 'morning coffee'. Hillingdon is no less sophisticated and Harefield is rapidly following suit.

Yet some of the countryside was being preserved, with 1,200 acres of open spaces in the Uxbridge urban district.

Suburban growth was a feature of the 1920s and 1930s, as it was for much of northern and western Middlesex, as some Londoners relocated from the dense city. In 1921, Uxbridge's population was 10,643; by 1951 it was 55,960. Ruislip-Northwood's growth was even higher; from 9,112 in 1921 to 68,238 in 1951. Between 1931 and 1961, Yiewsley and West Drayton's population nearly doubled to 23,723 by the latter date and Hayes's almost trebled, reaching 68,915 in 1961.

Council housing increased in this period. Yiewsley council had 246 houses built near Falling Lane for just over £100,000 in total. In Ruislip-Northwood 445 council houses had been built by 1939. Private housing also increased. The West Drayton Garden City included six-roomed houses for £450, though in Ruislip they were often nearly twice this. Publicity brochures stressed that these houses were 'a grand retreat for jaded city workers' and emphasized their rural aspect, despite the fact that their very building eroded the former considerably.

In 1938, there was the possibility of another World War and trenches and air-raids shelters began to be built in that year.

The Blitz of 1940–1 was less felt in these western suburbs than in central London, but 32 people were killed and 146 houses were destroyed in Ruislip and Northwood and another four people and seventeen houses were lost in the flying bomb attacks of 1944. In Uxbridge, several people were tragically killed by the bullets of an RAF fighter pursuing a German bomber. Uxbridge was the centre of No. 11 Fighter Group and information was sent from here in order to direct fighter aircraft in south-east England.

This part of Middlesex was traditionally Conservative, but as with many other places, the election of 1945 saw the dominance of the Labour Party. Frank Beswick, for instance, was the Labour MP for Uxbridge from 1945 to 1959. Another major feature of the post-war era was the establishment of Heathrow Airport, which opened in 1946. Although this provided employment and helped keep the rates in Yiewsley and West Drayton down, it also proved to be a major source of both pollution and noise. There was an American Air Force base in south Ruislip from 1949 to the 1970s and personnel came under suspicion when Jean Townsend was murdered nearby in 1954 (see Chapter 20).

Rapid growth of housing was not a general feature of the post-war world, because there was relatively little land to build upon, except in Yiewsley and West Drayton, and southwards expansion was curtailed because of Heathrow. Town-planning schemes in Uxbridge were well under way in the 1950s; government offices were built in Bakers Road, but much of the old town, such as the attractive Cross Street, was demolished.

CHAPTER 2

Law and Order in and around Uxbridge

I do not know why those should ever have been styled the 'good old days'. Sheer ignorance, without a doubt.... Indeed they were very bad, and we ought to be particularly thankful that we merely read about and do not live in them; for they were, in short, little more than times of battle, murder and sudden death. (Charles Harper, *Rural Nooks around London*, 1907)

Crime and disorder, like the poor, are constants in human societies, and this district is no different from any other. Crime is first recorded here in the sixteenth century. Lewis Jones of London stole clothes and other goods from Hugh Nevill of Uxbridge in 1571. These were valued at 25 shillings and Jones was hanged. Fifteen years later there was another incident which proved lethal. Five Uxbridge men were 'fighting together in the highway at Woxbridge [Uxbridge] with swords and staves. When John Bradley tried to stop them, he was hit over the head and slain.' Although no one was killed in the next example, which occurred in 1576, it was clearly seen as dangerous:

at Ruyslippe Co. Midd., Arthur Reynolds, husbandman … [and others] … all of Ruyslippe aforesaid, Thomas Darcye of Woxbridge yoman, and Thomas Davye taylor Roger Okeley, yoman, Thomas Harker husbandman, William Raynar, husbandman, and Richard Parsonne husbandman, all seven of Woxbridge aforesaid, with unknown malefactors to the number of a hundred, assembled themselves unlawfully and played a certain unlawful game, called football, by reason of which unlawful game, there rose amongst them a great affray, likely to result in homicides and serious accidents.

Criminal activity was not just the prerogative of the poor. In 1561, the Revd Peter Welthowe, vicar of Hillingdon, with a group of others, all armed, broke into John Newdegate's property at Harefield and damaged his crops and fields. Oddly enough, Welthowe was still vicar at Hillingdon until 1564.

Yet murder was uncommon. In 1602, John Pemmer, a gardener of West Drayton, 'administered in a potion a certain quantity of the powdered root of White Elebore to Anne, wife of Robert Fisher of Harlington'. He persuaded her it was a remedy for her sickness, so she took more and eventually died. He was not charged with murder because his victim had willingly taken it. A more serious charge was that against Elizabeth Roberts of West Drayton in 1601. She practised 'witchcraftes, enchauntments charmes and sorceries' on Richard Yerley, a 4 year old, who died. Three other children were also allegedly killed by her witchcraft. Oddly enough, these deaths occurred in the early 1590s, but she was not charged until later. The sentence passed is unknown, but witchcraft was then punishable by death.

Giles Hutson, writing in the late nineteenth century, recalled that there were a large number of burglaries in Uxbridge, and that drunkenness was common. He wrote, of brick makers and navvies, in the 1830s:

Money with these men at that time, at least during summer, was abundant, and their love of beer being great they indulged largely, and scenes of riot and violence were common. There being no police force many men were to be found on the following Sunday morning in

Did the West Drayton witch look like this?

the Market House or the neighbouring yards sleeping off the previous evening's debauch. It was no uncommon event for them to wake from their drunken sleep, get up and, if they had money left, go to the public house and then more drink ... Then they would quarrel and fight again.

The local forces to combat these crimes may seem pitifully inadequate. Since the Middle Ages, one or two constables were chosen to police each parish. In the early nineteenth century, two nightwatchmen were appointed in Uxbridge to supplement their efforts. They walked the streets at night, each armed with a heavy stick and carrying a lantern. They called out the time and the weather and visited public houses. All this gave any criminals advance warning of their presence, enabling them to flee. These nightwatchmen were figures of fun. Hutson recalled:

> on one occasion the watchman, enclosed in his box, was laid with the door of the box downwards where he had ignominiously to remain until some person passed by who was willing to assist him to get on his legs again. This watchbox was somewhat similar but not so substantial as the sentry boxes which are placed about government offices for the soldier on duty to retire to when the weather is bad, and was chained to the iron railings outside the Old Bank.

Other methods were used to deter crime. Shopkeepers patrolled the streets themselves, and they banded together to offer rewards for the capture of local villains. There was also the Uxbridge Volunteer Police Force, raised in 1836, which was under the control of the town's Watch Committee. This four-man unit; one sergeant and three constables, was housed in the old workhouse on Lynch Green. It appears that they were reasonably efficient at the task.

The major change to policing in this district, as in many others in Middlesex, came in 1840. A new Act of Parliament extended the Metropolitan Police district from London to cover all Middlesex and parts of other counties adjacent to the capital. The whole area was divided into divisions and the

Old Uxbridge Police Station, Windsor Road, 2007. Author's collection

parishes around Uxbridge were part of the Kilburn division (X). Initially the Uxbridge police station was on the corner of the Uxbridge Road and Kingston Lane. Edward Cook was the inspector in charge in 1845 and had two sergeants and two constables. In 1871 the purpose-built police station opened in Windsor Street, where it was to remain until 1988 (it is now a restaurant). By 1886, Inspector Christopher Brumfield was in command of two third-class inspectors, three sergeants and twenty-seven constables.

There was also a police presence in Ruislip and Hayes. Two police sergeants lived in a cottage on the Ickenham Road in 1845. They later moved to a house on the east side of Ruislip High Street in 1869. There was a stable at the back, where bicycles could be put. The house, purchased as a permanent building in 1871, was converted so as to include living accommodation for an inspector and a sergeant, as well as a charge room, parade room and cells. In 1886 Inspector Walter Weller was in charge at Ruislip, with two sergeants and eleven constables. At Hayes William Pimley was the inspector and had eleven men. In 1910 there was a police

New Uxbridge Police Station, Harefield Road, 2007. Author's collection

station in Northwood at Maxfield Road, and in 1917 there were two sergeants and eleven constables there. It was not thought necessary to have a police presence in Yiewsley and West Drayton until 1965 (ironically the station was built not far from the field where Carol White was killed in 1962). Before then, the police station at Harlington covered the district.

The importance of the uniformed police was that they were there to deter crime as much as to detect it. They were uniformed in blue and patrolled the streets, usually on foot, though sometimes on horseback. The rank-and-file constables carried a truncheon and a rattle, later a whistle, if aid was needed. Cutlasses could be issued in the early days and inspectors could carry revolvers. In many places, their introduction was seen as a worrying trend. First, they were under the direct control of the government in the shape of the Home Secretary. Older forms of policing had always been under local control. Furthermore, they were seen as expensive and even as potential tools of tyranny. It was not only the criminals who were concerned about their presence.

Hutson's assessment, from the perspective of 1884 was as follows:

> Although the introduction of the police was beneficial to private individuals and the public at large, yet the Uxbridge people were not satisfied, and incredible and unwise as such a course now appears, actually met in the vestry and resolved to remove the force from the town. Fortunately the authorities would not listen to the prayer of our forefathers on this subject and thus are now able to exist in comparative safety of life, limb and property.

A few words about the judicial system might be of use here. Once a crime had been identified as having been committed, the police were required to find evidence and witnesses in order to show who was responsible. Sometimes this was easy; as in the case of William Murray in 1869. But it was not always possible to find who was responsible, and a number of cases in this book were unsolved. This did not mean that the police necessarily did not know the truth, but that there was

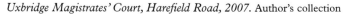

Uxbridge Magistrates' Court, Harefield Road, 2007. Author's collection

insufficient evidence to go before a court. Suspicion itself was not enough.

Up to the end of the nineteenth century, proof was difficult to come by. Unless the crime was witnessed or the criminal confessed, evidence was hard to find. Scientific aids were few. For example, fingerprinting was not used until the beginning of the twentieth century.

Once a suspect had been identified, he would appear before the Uxbridge magistrates. They would convene in a public house, or later the town hall, for the hearing, until the establishment of the court house at the bottom of Harefield Road in 1907. One petty criminal who was sentenced here in the 1930s, who gained notoriety in the 1950s, was one Reginald Christie. Here the witnesses would be assembled and evidence examined. If someone was identified as the likely suspect, he could, if proof seemed sufficient and if it was a serious offence, then be sent to the Central Criminal Court, commonly known as the Old Bailey, whose jurisdiction covered the whole of Middlesex and London. If the crime was murder or the lesser one of manslaughter, there would also

have to be an inquest, in order to ascertain the cause of death and, if possible, to pinpoint the culprit. In both cases, a jury was used to make the ultimate decision, though it was guided by the officials present. Inquests were usually held in public houses in the nineteenth century and before the county coroner or his deputy. The jury also had the unpleasant task of viewing the corpse.

At the Old Bailey, the accused would be on trial for

Metropolitan policeman, c. 1914.
Author's collection

Old Bailey, c. 1900. Author's collection

his life, if the crime was one of murder. Yet, even if found guilty, many did not suffer the ultimate penalty. Insanity would lead to a man keeping his life, and being detained elsewhere (often, since the mid-nineteenth century, Broadmoor), or the charge might be commuted to one of manslaughter. The number of killers who were executed was quite small, as this book will illustrate. Until the 1860s criminals could be transported, to the American colonies if before 1775, later to Australia; afterwards they could be given gaol sentences. The latter were unusual before then and gaols were used to hold prisoners prior to the trial. Hutson recalled:

> It was no unusual sight to observe a long stage coach loaded with twenty or thirty men in prison uniform chained together. These were convicts who had been sentenced to transportation at some of the assizes and were being moved from the country prisons to London prior to their embarkation to Botany Bay and Van Diemen's Land.

In later years, gaol sentences were the more common form of punishment for criminals, even those found guilty of murder.

CHAPTER 3

A Turbulent Priest, 1529–1534

By God's soul, thou art but a wretch, and it is pity thou
livest and that ever thou wert vicar here.

T he stereotypical image of the man of God as being
meek and mild is often far different from the reality.
Certainly, the Revd Henry Gold of Hayes was a
controversial figure. It is thought that he was born in St
Neot's, Huntingdonshire, in the late 1490s. He was first noted
as being in a chantry in St Peter's, Sandwich, in 1511. His
patron was the Archbishop of Canterbury, William Warham.
Gold graduated from the newly established St John's College,
Cambridge, in 1515, became a Fellow in 1516 and was
awarded an MA in 1518. He became a deacon and priest in
1520 and preached at the college.

Gold left Cambridge in 1525, being presented with a college
living at Ospringe in Kent. He did not stay long. In 1527 he

St John's College, Cambridge, c. 1912. Author's collection

joined Warham's household, becoming a chaplain. Two years later Warham presented him with two benefices: St Mary Aldermanbury in the City of London, and, more importantly, Hayes.

Gold began to live in Hayes as vicar (clergy did not have to reside in their parishes until much later). His brother, Thomas, farmed the rectory there. The two soon became involved in controversy. Thomas was a lawyer of the Middle Temple and was described as 'somewhat learned in the law and a man desirous of trouble and the vexation of his poor neighbours'. The root of the disputes was over tithes. Until the early nineteenth century, parishioners had to deliver a tenth of their produce to the rector in order to support the upkeep of the church. Many villagers resented this. During 1530, there was a major conflict between the Golds and their supporters and the bulk of the parishioners, led by Thomas Bradley and William Rowse.

Thomas Gold accused a leading villager, Bradley, 'the chief causer of the said great offences, misdemeanours and contempts', of preventing his fellow parishioners from laying out the tithe corn which was due to his brother. Apparently he had persuaded them to leave the rector's sheaves of corn still standing in the field, whilst taking their own, and so preventing the Golds from seeing if they had left the correct amount. Furthermore, the corn they left for the Golds was allegedly trampled down, or eaten, by the villagers' animals. In retaliation Gold's servants confiscated seventy-nine cattle and horses, as well as several pigs belonging to the villagers. His brother also accused Bradley of stopping people from making offerings at marriages and burials 'contrary to their old laudable customs to the great hurt and damages of the said Thomas Gold'. Problems also arose over cattle being given to the vicar as another form of tithe payment.

Other parishioners were criticized by the Golds. Rowse, the constable, was also an innkeeper. He was accused of allowing people to play illegal games there, such as cards and football. One card player was the aforementioned Bradley and he had made great gains at cards. Yet all this evidence came from Peter Lee, the curate, whose repute was a dubious one, for he was accused of consorting with rogues. Although Gold had been told by Warham to dismiss him, he refused. Gold had also been advised by the churchwardens to dismiss Thomas Troughton, the parish clerk, for 'his evil demeanour'. Again Gold refused. Gold was accused of having 'smote the said William Rowse upon the breast'.

Not all the faults were on the Golds' side, it must be admitted. Rowse had been derelict in his duty in failing to prevent unlawful outdoor games, such as tennis, bowls, quoits and football – the latter game being, of course, accompanied by violence. Rowse also failed to arrest one Richard Page, who appeared to be a burglar, entering the large houses in the parish such as Hayes Park Hall. Although Rowse finally arrested him, Page escaped very soon afterwards and so some collusion between the two seems probable.

The conflict escalated as time went by. Even church services became the focus of physical violence. Gold was threatened during one service. Apparently Bradley said to Gold, 'By God's soul, thou art but a wretch, and it is pity thou livest and that ever thou wert vicar here.' In another, parishioners arrived armed with cudgels. Matters were clearly serious, for the churchwardens removed the church silver and so the service had to be cancelled.

Hayes Parish Church, c. *1900.* Author's collection

One contemporary commentator alleged of Gold, 'He also says that the inhabitants conspire his death, and that he knew it by a maid who was servant with Henry King.' Yet 'Gold once spoke to her in the house of Mr Dewer and promised he would give her a years wages if she would testify against them, and that she should come and be with him'. For a theoretically celibate priest, this was a strong accusation to make.

It was so serious that the dispute was sent to the Star Chamber Court in 1531–2 for settlement. Usually this court only dealt with very serious and weighty matters, not parochial squabbles. The latter at Hayes ranked with the mighty affairs of the law.

Unfortunately, we do not know how this ended. Preparations for the trial began in August 1531, with evidence taken from all parties, a lengthy procedure which was not finished until October. Some of the Golds' enemies were sent to the Fleet Prison in London awaiting trial, but we do not know how long they stayed there. Legally the Golds were mainly in the right, but they were seen as being greedy, high-handed and tactless in their dealings with the parishioners. Elsewhere in the diocese, the clergy were less forceful in demanding their rights, but the Golds did not believe in such tolerance.

In any case, by then, the Golds' attention was elsewhere. They decided to become involved with the 'Holy Maid of Kent'. This was Elizabeth Barton (1506–34). Elizabeth had been a farm servant in Kent, working for a tenant of the archbishop. In 1525, she had visions and made predictions, mostly of a religious nature. These brought her fame. In the following year, she entered the Benedictine priory of St Sepulchre, Canterbury, and took her vows in 1527. Edward Bocking, a monk, became her confessor. Many people travelled to see her, to seek her intercession for the sick, the dying and the dead. However, in 1530, she entered the political arena and made a most contentious prophecy:

> that in case hys Highnes proceded to the accomplishment of the seid devorce and married another, that then hys Majestie shulde not be kynge of this Realme by the space of one

moneth after. And in the reputacion of God shuld not be kynge one day nor one houre.

This came at a very politically sensitive time. Henry VIII was seeking a divorce from his first wife, Catherine of Aragon, and he was prepared to go to extreme steps in order to do so. Anyone who stood in his way was treading a very dangerous path indeed.

Warham supported her and so did Henry Gold. The latter was very attached to her. He wrote, 'I intend to be with her again this day three weeks, and so to be monthly, so long as God shall please.' He also wrote to her as, 'My lover, my sister, my earthly comfort'. He sought her help on behalf of his friend, Mr White, who was diseased, who 'desireth you … to make meekly petition to God for the knowledge thereof'. The Gold brothers spread her revelations far and wide, among clergy, monks, merchants and even, apparently, Queen Catherine herself. Thomas wanted his children 'brought up by her in virtue and learning'. We do not know the Golds' motivations nor their exact relationship with Elizabeth. Certainly Gold seemed to hold her in high esteem at the very least. In 1532–3, Gold and his sister-in-law visited Elizabeth in London each month.

Yet Warham died in 1532 and when Thomas Cranmer became archbishop in 1533, the whole situation changed. Cranmer was the King's man and was determined to assist his master against his enemies. Cranmer led an investigative commission against Barton. She confessed that she was a fraud and her visions were imaginary. She was forced to recant in public in November 1533. As supporters of her cause, the Golds also suffered. By November 1533, both were incarcerated in the Tower. In January 1534, it was noted that 'Many persons were ready to preach her revelations' and later confessed, and Gold was among their number. He was accused of spreading sedition against the King, being 'most busy to sow this mischievous seed abroad with great craft and secret conveyance'.

Gold would not speak against Elizabeth herself and was condemned to death in March. However, he decided he would need to change his tack in order to try and save his brother. Gold wrote to Thomas Cromwell, another of the King's ministers, 'I desire you will have compassion on my poor brother, who was miserably deceived by that false and dissembling Nun, like as I and others were.'

On 20 April 1534, Barton was executed alongside Henry Gold and others in London, being hung and then beheaded. Gold was buried in the churchyard of his London parish. His head was put on a spike on London Bridge. Thomas was luckier. Though deprived of his property at Hayes, he was only imprisoned, and in 1536 was released, securing a pardon.

Gold had led a turbulent and controversial life, and perhaps had not known when to be prudent. Crossing swords with his parishioners was one thing, but to do the same with the King was another. Yet he does not seem to have been aiming at martyrdom.

CHAPTER 4

The Uxbridge Martyrs, 1555

*At length he being well-nigh half-burnt, and all black with
fire, clustered together as in a lump like a black coal.*

We have already seen how religious and political
turmoil cost men their lives. After Henry VIII died
in 1547, he was succeeded by his young son,
Edward VI, under whom the Protestant revolution was pushed
further. However, his short reign and life ended in 1553.
Mary, Henry's eldest daughter, became queen to, at first,
much popular rejoicing.

Devoutly religious herself, her mission was to return
England to the Catholic fold. One tactic in this mission was to
force Protestants to recant, and if they remained obdurate, to
have them tried and executed by burning. Such tactics were
common on the Continent and had also been used in England
in earlier epochs. As well as prominent figures, such as
Archbishop Cranmer and a number of bishops, more lowly
men and women were also caught in the deadly net. The
campaign began in 1555 and did not cease until Mary's death
three years later. The men who died at Uxbridge were thus
among the first to become martyrs.

We do not know why Uxbridge was chosen as a place of
execution. None of the three men even came from Middlesex,
as far as is known. It is likely that the town was chosen because
it was a prominent place in the county, where many people
would see the executions and would thus hopefully profit from
the example. Brentford was chosen in 1558 for another round
of burnings, doubtless for the same reason. Also, if the martyrs
were burnt far away from where their friends and relations
lived, sympathy for them might be reduced.

One of the martyrs was John Denley. He and a friend, John
Newman, both of whom lived in Maidstone, were travelling to

Martyrs' Memorial, Uxbridge, 2007. Author's collection

Essex to visit friends. Once in that county, they met one Edmund Tyrell 'a justice of the peace within the county of Essex, an assister to cruel murderers of God's saints'. Tyrell stopped the men and had them searched. He found Protestant writings on them. This was enough to have them sent to the Queen's commissioners. The latter were unable to make the two men change their faith.

It was on 23 June that Denley, plus Patrick Packingham, an itinerant workman, were brought before the Bishop of London, John Bonner. He examined them and urged them to recant. This had no effect. Denley told him, 'God save me from your counsel and keep me in the mind that I am in, for that you count heresy I take to be the truth.' They were then told to appear at the consistory court on 5 July.

On 1 July, Bonner tried other tactics. He read them their confessions and answers, tempted them to recant, made promises, but most of all, he made threats. Nothing could alter their stance. Finally, on 5 July, at the consistory court hearing, they were condemned as heretics and passed over to the sheriffs for punishment.

Denley was sent to Uxbridge and the date for his execution was 8 August. When the wood was lit, he began to sing a psalm. This provoked Dr Story, a Catholic professor of law who was in the audience, to try and silence him by commanding a man to hurl a faggot at him, which he did. The missile hit its target and Denley bled. He clapped his hands to his face, momentarily ceasing his singing. Story said 'Truly, thou hast marred a good old song'. But the last word was with Denley, and in the chronicler's words, 'still in the flame of the fire, put his hands abroad and sung again, yielding at last his spirit into the hands of God'.

Robert Smith was the second of the trio of Uxbridge martyrs. He was a poet and painter from Windsor. Whilst he was in prison awaiting trial, he wrote to his wife and others, and his writings were full of piety and courage: 'Love all men but especially your enemies ... Bring up your children and yours in the fear of God, and then shall I not fail but receive you in everlasting kingdom of God, which I go into.'

His death at Uxbridge on 8 August was grim:

> so now, also being at the stake, he did no less comfort the people, there standing about him, willing them to think well of his cause, and not to doubt that his body dying in that quarrel, should rise again to life. And said he, I doubt not but that God will shew you some token thereof ... At length he being well-nigh half-burnt, and all black with fire, clustered together as in a lump like a black coal, all even thinking him for dead, suddenly rose upright before the people, lifting up the stumps of his arms and clapping the same together, declaring a rejoicing heart unto them, and so bending down again, and hanging over the fire, slept in the Lord and ended his mortal life.

Packingham was charged by Bonner for not taking off his cap during mass at the bishop's chapel on 23 June. He also refused to receive holy water and bread blessed by the priests, saying he despised such rituals. This was deemed a heinous offence. Although Packingham was urged to recant, he refused to do so and said that he believed that there was no Catholic Church, but the church of Satan. He was taken to Uxbridge later in the month and was burnt at the stake there on 28 August.

These deaths were far worse than they might have been. On the Continent, victims were either killed first or gunpowder was placed among the faggots, ensuring a quicker death. Few burnt to death, but the executioners in England were inexperienced and unskilful in such practices. In any case, all these burnings were counterproductive. England, by and large, did not mourn Mary's death in 1558, but welcomed her successor, the Protestant Elizabeth. Mary had earned for herself the unwelcome epithet 'Bloody Mary' and the Protestant cause continued to benefit by reference to the burnings for centuries. It is a pity that the reactions of local people to these events are unknown. However, in 1642, the town seemed solid behind the Parliamentary cause, which was anti-Catholic. In August 1955, a monument was erected to the martyrs in the now redundant parish churchyard in Uxbridge. It reads:

> This stone was erected in August 1955 in memory of Robert Smith, John Denley & Patrick Packingham who were burnt at the stake on Lynch Green opposite this spot in August 1555 and also of all those men and women of Uxbridge who have suffered persecution in their Christian faith.

As to Story, he fell out of favour in the following reign. He was involved with Catholic plotters who, following the Pope's lead, aimed to replace Elizabeth with a Catholic monarch. He was executed in 1571. Had he not ordered a missile to be thrown at Denley at Uxbridge, he would have been subsequently canonized.

CHAPTER 5

Marital Strife in Harefield, 1784

*You wicked man, to go to lay your revenge upon
your poor wife.*

illiam Walker was charged at the Old Bailey for
attacking Ann Walker, his wife, in Harefield
with a certain clasp knife, of the value of twopence, which he
in his right hand then and there held, in and upon the breast
of the said Ann, did strike, stab, thrust, giving the said Ann
in and upon the breast of the said Ann, with the clasp knife
aforesaid, one mortal wound of the length of one inch, and
of the breadth of three inches, of which she instantly died.

The court noted, in its stereotypical fashion, that Walker's
crime was due to his 'not having the fear of God before his
eyes, but being moved and seduced by the instigation of the
Devil'.

The Walkers, with their two infant children, had not long
lived in the small village of Harefield. He was a labourer,
employed by Mr Horne, in threshing work in his barn. Walker
seemed an ordinary enough fellow. His neighbour, Joseph
Branch, referred to him as 'A very good sort of a man all that
I saw' and certainly one who was always sober, drinking no
more than a pint in any one session at the village's two inns.
Walker's other neighbour, Francis Jones, agreed that this was
so. No one had any inkling that a tragedy was in the making.

Ann Walker was the only one who could sense any danger.
On Monday 1 March 1784, she asked Edward Trumper, the
constable, to speak to her husband and to ask him what the
matter was; she had had no success. Trumper accordingly
inquired and Walker replied, in a vague manner, 'I do not
know, I am very much troubled, but I do not know what is the

The King's Arms, Harefield, 2007. Author's collection

reason of it.' Trumper suggested that he return to work and to
see if that helped. Ann also asked Samuel Wood to tell Mr
Morton, the parish overseer, 'because she was afraid to be in
the house when there was nobody else in the house but they
and the children'. However, Morton did not visit her.

On Thursday 4 March, Jones had been at Wood's and Ann
asked him, 'Will you be so good to come and sit in our house?'
He had agreed and, on arrival, witnessed the following scene
between man and wife. Walker asked Ann, 'Nan, what do you
mean by leaving me to myself? You be not afraid of a man?'
Ann said that she was not and he told her to come to bed and
was told that she had invited Jones around. Walker replied,
'Let any body come, I do not care who comes'. He then locked
the door and announced, presumably to Jones, 'I want to settle
affairs with my wife and she will not resolve me'. She declared
'she would resolve him anything that he asked her'. Then she
accompanied him upstairs.

On her return, Walker remaining upstairs in bed, she found
that Wood and Ann Priest had arrived at her house. She then
told them an unsettling tale. Apparently, her husband 'had
drawn his knife upon her six weeks ago in bed'. Last night he

had told her 'he would give her time to say her prayers and then he would kill her'. Ann could not say why he wanted to kill her, and why he did not do so.

She then went next door. Branch was a man who believed in keeping his neighbours at arm's length, stating: 'I never go to anybody's house but to my own, and that is best'. So it doubtless came as a surprise to him that Ann asked him to pay a visit. He had never entered their house before. He recalled that she asked 'if I would come and sit there, I should feel so glad'. He recalled, 'it was something odd to be sure, I could give no account about it' and thought that Ann was 'a good sort of woman'. This was no illicit assignation, for she added that 'her husband would not meddle with her, if there was somebody in the house'. Branch followed her and on arrival saw that Jones and Wood were also there, in the lower room.

Walker came downstairs and addressed the men there, 'What my lads!' then he went back upstairs. Eventually Ann followed him. Branch and Jones heard fragments of their conversation. Jones recalled, that she said 'do not make yourself uneasy, they will be paid, I warrant you'. Walker replied, 'Nan you must satisfy them'. She then said, 'do not make yourself uneasy, go to sleep, if you can. You have not had any a good while; Mr Morton will satisfy them.' Branch recalled Ann asking her husband, 'Are you going to get up?' Walker said 'No.' Ann said. 'Do you want the pot?' Her husband said he did not.

After this conversation, there was a scream. Ann fell down the steps and her husband tried to stamp on her. In his right hand he held a bloodstained knife. They were only dressed in shirt and shift. Branch went for the constable and recalled, 'I saw no more'.

Walker told Jones, 'I meant to kill her, now I am easy, now I shall be hanged, and wish to die.' His wife lay dying, but she was able to utter some last words, 'O Lord, have mercy upon me. Where be O going next, the matter with my head.' Walker addressed her, 'Nan, what, beest dead? I told thee how I would serve thee, but thee wouldst not be ruled, you nasty, dirty hussy.'

Walker then went to the drawers and found handkerchiefs and keys. He threatened no one else. It was between two and three o'clock. Branch arrived at Trumper's house and told him, 'Walker has killed his wife'. Trumper went to the house and found the dying woman supported by Ann Priest. He addressed Walker, 'What have you done? You have killed your wife.' He replied, 'She deserved it, she has used me ill, I am not sorry for it.' Trumper went for a surgeon, but it was already too late. There were three stab wounds in her chest and another in her side. Walker tamely allowed himself to be handcuffed. Ann Priest told him, 'You wicked man, to go to lay your revenge upon your poor wife.'

Trumper took Walker to Mr Fellow's house; presumably he was the nearest JP. At eight that morning, Walker was escorted to Uxbridge, doubtless to be examined by other magistrates. On 8 March the inquest was held and, soon after, Walker was taken to Newgate to await trial for murder.

At the trial it was found that Walker's violent tendencies had been apparent before the killing. One woman said that he had killed his cat with an axe. Morton the overseer came in for censure. Oddly enough, he was not asked to give evidence. But it was stated that he might have been able to have prevented the tragedy if he had investigated Ann's fears. He might have been able to arrange for medicine or taken other steps. There were also doubts cast upon Walker's sanity. As was noted at the trial, 'this was the unhappy effect of rage against the woman, conceived in consequences of distemper of mind, brought on by disease, and that when that impression, the violence was committed'.

Walker was found not guilty of murder, by reason of his insanity. His fate is uncertain. He could not be discharged from gaol, unless proper care was taken of him by the parish officials. He was consigned to Bedlam, as there was no asylum for insane paupers in Middlesex until the one founded in Norwood in 1831, and the parish made payments for his upkeep. Eventually he was transferred from there to a private asylum, where he died shortly afterwards.

Walker was suffering from delusions. Perhaps he was suffering from schizophrenia. He clearly saw his wife as his enemy. Unfortunately she did not receive the help she expected from Morton. Yet it is unlikely that he would have been able to assist her.

CHAPTER 6

A Regency Whodunit, 1816

> The Coroner … said that he never knew of a more
> shocking occurrence.

Mr William Howard was described as being 'a respectable farmer, 90 years of age'. In 1816 he lived in Yiewsley, in the same house as he had done for nearly sixty years. The chief produce of the farm was hay, which was sold at London's Haymarket by William Baker of Kilburn. Howard was of good health, but was a little deaf. He was a widower (he and his late wife, Martha, had had three children – Sarah, Elizabeth and Mary), though he had an elderly housekeeper, Sarah Randall (1740–1824), who had been his servant for forty years. His grandson, John Bond (1771–1839), lived with him, and helped work the farm. Thomas Hayes was another employee who lived in. No servant had been discharged in the last three years; it was evidently a stable little household. Other members of his family lived nearby. One such was Thomas Bond, John's brother, who lived and worked at John Austin's about a mile and a half away.

John Bond had been working in the fields that Sunday afternoon of 1 December 1816. He then was at Thomas Wyman's house and left at about 6.30. He came home at about 7 and made a dreadful discovery. The place was in darkness – normally it would have been lit by candle light. Sarah spoke to him in the darkness. He found a candle and after lighting it, surveyed the scene:

> I saw the deceased, my grandfather, sitting in his armchair, as he usually did; his face was dreadfully bruised, his eyes were beaten nearly out of their sockets, and blood was pouring from his head and eyes over his small clothes, and

he was nearly covered. Sarah Randall was also very bloody and could scarcely speak.

It was shortly after 7 that John Bond entered the Trout to tell the terrible news, saying 'Come some of you, for someone has nearly murdered the old people'. It was later noted that Bond was wearing the same clothing (a white smock) as he had been when he left Wyman's. Men rushed to the scene of the crime. He recalled his grandfather's last words. These were 'Pray don't, it is very cold', when Bond tried to wash his face. Then he said to Sarah, 'Oh Sarah'. He never spoke again. Another witness reported that Howard said 'Oh! John, don't hurt me'. Howard's chair had been facing the door, so he could have seen anyone enter.

Mr John Curtis of Cowley was a surgeon and his assistance was called for that evening. He arrived at about eight and later recalled:

> I came to his house and, upon examining his head, I found that he had received three distinct blows which had been given by some blunt instrument which had caused a concussion of the brain, and an internal fracture of the skull. In consequence of the blows he had received he was quite insensible; he had lost a great quantity of blood, and never spoke. I am perfectly satisfied that the deceased died from the effects of the blows which he had received. He died on Monday afternoon at three o'clock: he never moved, except from compulsive spasms, after he was put to bed.

Sarah Randall's head had been split open in the centre of the scalp and had bled heavily. Her throat had also been injured. Curtis did not think she would recover. She was able to give him a little information about the murder. She had been sitting by the fire with Howard, who was smoking a pipe. She never saw the intruders, as her chair had its back to the door. However, she survived the assault and reported that she remembered hearing the door unlatched and then she suffered several blows. She begged for mercy, but no one else spoke and someone grabbed her throat.

Upstairs the place was a mess. The bureau had been rifled of money. Howard's will was found and it appeared to have been opened by someone with bloody hands. The bureau had been locked, but the key may have been in Howard's pockets, because someone had been through them. Bond later said he never went upstairs after he found the two below. A bloodstained candle was found in the cellar below.

At the inquest on Wednesday 4 December, held at the Trout (this pub once stood by the canal at the end of Trout Lane but is now demolished), Thomas Haynes gave some intriguing testimony. He had been in Mr Howard's employ. At 5.45 on the evening of the murder, he was waiting by the canal bridge for a friend before going to the pub. His friend did not arrive, so Haynes walked to the pub past the lane which led to his master's house. He recalled:

> I saw a stranger about forty yards from the house, walking towards me, but he avoided me, and instead of walking over the bridge he walked through the water. I said to him, 'Mate, you have missed your way'; he did not answer at first, and when he did he was apparently confused, and said, 'Ah! I know'. The man walked on and I went to the Trout public house.

Haynes described the stranger thus, 'about 5 feet 6 inches in height, he appeared to be dressed in working dress, he had light smallclothes on, a large hat, a red handkerchief, and a fustian jacket, a white bundle under his arm, and a great stick in his hand'. Search was made for this man later in the evening of 1 December. But he was never seen again. William Mercer and Thomas Ayres also reported that they had seen a stranger in the vicinity, but were not close enough to identify him.

The coroner said he would apply to Lord Sidmouth, the Home Secretary, for a reward to be offered for the apprehension of the killer. Meanwhile, the jury returned a verdict of murder by person or persons unknown. John Bond said 'I have no suspicion who it could be.' Theft was probably the motive, though, for the house had been rifled and money had probably been stolen. It was thought that there might have

St John the Baptist's Church, Hillingdon, c. *1800s.* Author's collection

been between £200 and £300 there, as well as valuable plate.

A reward poster offered £100 for the apprehension of the criminals; half of which was offered by the family and the other half by Hillingdon vestry (at this time, Yiewsley was part of the parish of Hillingdon).

Howard was buried on 8 December, at St John's church, Hillingdon, the parish register reading that he 'was cruelly robbed and murdered in his own house'. His will was read shortly afterwards. It had been made by the illiterate old man on 27 December 1813 before Thomas Riches, an Uxbridge solicitor. He had certainly been a wealthy man. Apparently, John Bond and Joseph Allen, a local farmer, were to be trustees of the bulk of the estate, namely £2,000 invested in stock at the Bank of England, which yielded a 3 per cent annual return. This money was to be split between two of Howard's married daughters; Sarah Bond (1751–1820), who lived in Yiewsley, and Elizabeth Whitfield who lived in Surrey. A granddaughter, Ann Barnes, of Andover, was given £250 worth of stock. Joseph Simmonds of Surrey was also to receive £250 of stock. John Bond and Sarah Randall were to receive £50 each. Any remaining money and goods were to be equally shared between the six beneficiaries. Did these people know the contents of the will? Could they have guessed? Did the will provide a motive for any of them? Sarah and John Bond lived nearby and both benefited.

However, in the summer of the following year, suspicion fell on John Bond. He had had changed for him a £10 note, numbered 10,108 and dated 30 April 1816, at Uxbridge bank. It was proved that this note had been in his grandfather's possession in the previous year. Bond was charged with robbery and murder and was sent for trial at the Old Bailey. Yet Sarah Bond, his mother, said that she had found the money in the secret drawer of a bureau which her late father once owned, and had subsequently passed to her, and then to her son, who was owed £30. Bond was therefore discharged.

Bond found himself in danger again, in 1839, as was his brother, Thomas. By now he was reduced to living in the Hillingdon Workhouse, was very infirm and walked with a stick. Thomas, on the other hand, had fared better and looked like a well-to-do middle-aged farmer. One George Haynes, a well-known criminal of Hillingdon, had been sentenced to transportation for life for sheep stealing. In order to try and earn a reprieve, he offered to provide information about the murder of Mr Howard. The magistrates made no promises, but Charles Murray, High Constable of Uxbridge, visited him in his cell in Newgate on 16 April for further information.

Haynes claimed that he had been sleeping near Howard's house on the afternoon of the murder and then woke at about 7. He saw two men; John Bond and his brother Thomas, armed with stout sticks, and wearing smocks. Haynes heard the following snatch of conversation between the two brothers. John said,

> What had we better do with the old – ; shall we murder him?
> – Yes, we had better murder him, and then he can tell no one.
> – What shall we do it with; we have nothing but this stick.
> – There is a good bar to the door and that will do.

They then allegedly entered the house and Haynes said that he had heard the old man cry out 'oh dear'.

Both brothers denied that Haynes spoke the truth. Thomas said that he was at Gerrard's Cross on the night of the murder and did not know about it until the following day. William Hatch, a Hanworth farmer, recalled having met Thomas near Gerrard's Cross at 6.45 on the evening of the crime. Sir William Wiseman, the chief magistrate, said that in view of Haynes's notorious character and the fact that his evidence was uncorroborated, he should not be relied on. The brothers were set free. John died later that year, aged 68.

Who did kill Howard? Presumably robbery was the motive? In the economic depression following the end of the Napoleonic wars, there was great deal of unemployment and poverty, and many men, having served in the armed forces but now jobless, who knew how to kill and had already done so. Possibly one or more of them took the opportunity of finding a house containing two defenceless people who possibly had valuables. Perhaps the man seen by Thomas Haynes was the killer? Or perhaps one or more of the Howard family were responsible? The stranger who had been seen might have been merely an innocent bystander and his being near the crime scene a coincidence. Could Sarah and John have been involved, either separately or jointly? They could easily have surprised the old man and would have been interested in the contents of the will, whereas a common criminal who would probably have been illiterate, would not have been. Perhaps neither spoke prior to the assault because their voices might have been recognized? It seems we shall never know the truth.

CHAPTER 7

Horrid and Mysterious Murder near Uxbridge, 1837

I'd sooner be taken for the murder than to go to prison for this.

In about December 1836, John Brill, a 15 year old employed by Charles Churchill, a Harefield farmer, had given evidence in a poaching case heard before the magistrates at Uxbridge. His evidence had helped to prove the guilt of Thomas Lavender and James Bray. These men, and their friends, threatened him with violence. Brill lived in Ruislip with his parents; his father was a labourer.

Two months later Brill went missing. He had left his father's house at 5.45 am on Thursday 16 February 1837 as usual. At 10, his master told him to fix some gaps in the hedges by Young's Wood, which was by the road between Uxbridge and Rickmansworth, and now part of Mad Bess Wood. He never returned home after work. A search was begun in Young's Wood that night, 'but no trace of him could be discovered'. On the following day, all of Churchill's men were sent to find him, looking in all directions. Yet this was fruitless. The search continued on Saturday, but again he could not be found. Young's Wood was fairly impenetrable, with thick undergrowth, five feet high, few paths, except for those used by animals, and 'a place well adapted for the perpetration of any atrocious crime without the chance of immediate detection'.

It was only on Sunday morning, when more people were drafted into help, that a discovery was made. Oddly enough, it was James Lavender, the father of the man whom Brill had helped to convict, who made the discovery. Apparently he had been reluctant to take part in the search. His wife had said to

Young's Wood, Ruislip, 2007. Author's collection

him, 'Why don't you go and look after that poor boy, it looks so unneighbourly.' He replied, 'Very well, I might as well go for an hour or so.' The corpse of Brill was found in a hollow in a remote part of the wood about a quarter of an hour later. According to a newspaper report:

> When found he was lying on his back, quite dead. His clothes were quite in disorder, and his face was covered in dirt, as if he had been rolled in the decayed leaves with which the spot was covered.

Lavender called out and soon others had joined him. They examined the body.

> the marks of a severe blow were discovered under the right ear, which was considerably swollen, and from which a quantity of blood had flowed. About six yards behind him, the bill-hook which he had been using was found, and on a hedge just above him was his cap, which had apparently been caught by the furze as he fell. There were also marks in

The Six Bells Pub. Author's collection

the leaves as far as five or six yards, as if the deceased had staggered before he fell.

The body was stiff and the neck appeared to be broken. The corpse was taken to the Six Bells in Ruislip, to await a coroner's inquest.

Two days later, the examination began. James Brill, the father of the deceased, said that the place his son had been found was close to a blind path used by hares and also close to a footpath. Three suspects were rounded up two days later: Charles Lamb, Thomas Lavender and James Bray.

Charles Lamb was a 35-year-old labourer, whose 'countenance was of an ashy paleness and he exhibited symptoms of great depression of spirits'. He was handcuffed. He attested his innocence. Thomas Lavender was about 24, and also a labourer. He did not seem downhearted and merely remarked that he was innocent. James Bray was the last of the trio; also a labourer, aged 25. As with Lamb, he 'was exceedingly pale, his lips being quite bloodless'.

Witnesses were then called. Henry Meadows, gamekeeper to Mr Dean, recalled that at 7 on Sunday evening, a man whom the court did not wish to be identified in public had come to his cottage, but Meadows was not in. However, he saw him not far away. The man said 'I want to speak to you very particularly', but then hesitated and said nothing. He turned away, but then asked 'Shall you be home tomorrow morning?' Meadows replied that he would be. The man returned and told him that he could prove that Lamb had been seen coming out of the wood on the evening of Brill's disappearance. Lamb said this was untrue.

Meadows added that the killer must be one of the three suspects, who had previously threatened Brill, alleging that they would 'whip him up to a tree some day or other'. He also related a conversation in the Six Bells on Sunday morning. Thomas Lavender had remarked, on hearing that Lamb had joined in the search for the lad, that he was 'a b–y fool for doing so, as the boy's mother had said that he (the prisoner), Charles Lamb, and James Bray, had killed the deceased, and that if he could catch hold of her, he would kick her – till the blood ran from her nose'.

Rachel Brill, the lad's mother, denied that she had said this. She had had no suspicion of who had killed her son. But she did recall that shortly after her son had given evidence at the poaching case that a lad called Henry Hill told Mary, her daughter, that Jack should take care of himself because James Bray had said he would murder him when he had the chance.

Mr Wiseman, a magistrate, announced that there was no doubt that 'a most atrocious murder' had been committed and that everyone should help to bring its perpetrators to justice. The prisoners were remanded in custody and were sent, separately, to the cages at Uxbridge, Hillingdon and Ickenham, where they had been confined on the previous night.

The examination continued on the following day. Mary Hill, who lived on Ruislip Common, said that she had seen Lamb on Thursday morning, between 10 and 11. He had been walking towards Young's Wood. Later that day, on her way to her grandmother's, at about noon, she had again seen him, leaving the wood, with a bundle of sticks under his arm. Mary Brill confirmed her mother's early statement, adding that Hill had told her 'Tell Jack to look out, for Jem Bray says he'll kill him as soon as he has an opportunity' and when she told this to her brother, he remarked, 'he did not care for Jem Bray'. Hill denied he had said these words.

The suspects were then brought forward. They pleaded their innocence again. Lamb, however, agreed that what Hill had said was correct. He said that on the Thursday, he had been walking between various fields and had met various persons, though he could not remember their names. However Bray said that George Alliday and Thomas Godliman could vouch for his movements on that day.

Suspicion was directed towards Lamb as he had been seen in the vicinity of the crime on the day of the lad's disappearance. Yet this did not absolve the others. It was possible that Brill had been taken prisoner on Thursday and killed on Friday or Saturday, as the body had not been found until Sunday. The time of death could not be ascertained. All the suspects were remanded again.

Despite these suspicions, there was no firm evidence against any of the three men, though Lamb seemed the most likely suspect. He had motive and opportunity. The inquest on 23 February did not unearth any additional facts and so they were all discharged. Curiously enough, Bray asked that he could see the body of the deceased 'as he had suffered a good deal through him'. This could have been because he thought that, by doing so, he would impress others with his innocence, 'there being a superstition among the uneducated classes that the blood of the murdered person will burst out if the murderer approached the body'. Lamb and Lavender also saw the body and again said that they were innocent.

The Ruislip churchwardens wrote to the Home Secretary, Lord Russell, on 5 March 1837, to 'solicit your lordship to offer a reward to apprehend the murderer or murderers of John Brill'. The government issued posters advertising that anyone who could successfully identify the guilty party would receive £100 on conviction, and another £50 if they could apprehend him. Alas, this method had no success.

The matter might have remained so, despite further efforts being made to discover the killer, had not one of the prisoners been remarkably indiscreet to a fellow criminal a few years later.

On Christmas Eve of 1844, Sir William Wiseman, an Uxbridge magistrate, received a letter. It was from Mr Chesterton, the governor of Cold Bath Field House of Correction in London. Part of it read:

> Sir, – a voluntary declaration has this day been made to me by a prisoner named George Sibley, the younger, who was committed to this prison by you on the 14th of October last, to the effect that Charles Lamb, also a prisoner, committed by you on the 14th of October last, had told him (Sibley) that about a fortnight before their committal, one afternoon between 4 and 5 o' clock, when on the road from Rickmansworth to Harefield, a few years since, he (Lamb) had killed a lad, named John Brill, in Mr Churchill's wood at Ruislip; that he struck the lad with a stick, and when he lay on the ground he took the lad's cap and hung it on a tree, to make it appear he had fallen out of the tree; and he took the lad's bill-hook and glove lying near the body. Sibley says, that Charles Lamb had warned him, that if he said anything about it, it should be the worse for him.

The governor added that Sibley had asked to be set free because of this information, which Chesterton thought to be very suspicious. He also asked Lamb if he knew anyone by the name of John Brill. Lamb said he had been charged with his murder, but was not guilty. Chesterton was not convinced about Sibley's veracity, but thought he should pass on the information, for what it was worth, to Wiseman.

Wiseman thought that the case should be reopened. He summoned a meeting of magistrates and on 28 December they went to the prison and took a statement from Sibley. The prisoner recounted his earlier story and added that he thought Lamb needed to unburden himself to someone because he had been having 'such queer dreams'. He then made his mark on the statement.

The magistrates then wrote a letter to the Home Secretary to allow Lamb to be taken to Uxbridge. They added that

Lamb was a habitual prisoner, who had been a sheep stealer and a poacher, and had already served four years for theft. Yet they received a disappointing reply. Lamb could not be removed from his present place of incarceration, but they could visit the prison and examine Lamb and Sibley there. There was much local excitement in Uxbridge and witnesses who had given their evidence in 1837 were again asked to recollect it.

In February 1845, Lamb was on trial for Brill's murder at the Old Bailey. Sibley was the principal witness and recounted what Lamb had told him; namely, on passing the wood the previous year, 'I'd sooner be taken for the murder than to go to prison for this' (i.e. poaching). He told how Lamb had threatened to kill him if he told anyone about what he had just told him. Lamb protested his innocence. He said that Sibley knew that he had been accused of the murder in 1837 as he lived locally too, but that his confession was a mere invention. The trial was postponed until the next day.

On Saturday 8 February, at 10 am, the case opened. Lamb pleaded 'not guilty'. Additional information was given by Churchill. He said that he had told Brill to see if anyone tried to steal wood from his property and, if so, to get a good look at the thief, before running back to report it to him. He was to take his lunch at 1 at the farmer's house. Churchill had seen the lad at his work at 10.30, then went to market. On his return, at about 3, he was surprised to find that Brill was not at the farm, as he was ordinarily. He then went to the wood to look for him, but without success, so went to the lad's parents' house.

James Lavender then explained how he had found the corpse so quickly. He explained that all the others went in one direction, whereas he went in another. 'This is not the way I went a bird-nesting when I was a boy.' Brill's father stated that his son had been 'a good-tempered, inoffensive boy'.

Other witnesses repeated their evidence, one such being Mary Allday (nee Hill). Charles Woodman, a farmer, recalled seeing Brill at 11 am on 16 February. Henry Woodman recalled seeing Lamb on that day near to the wood, and Lamb had asked him if he had seen Churchill or his wife go to market that day. John Bray recalled seeing Lamb walking quickly from the wood, and then saw him in the Six Bells, where he drank beer.

Although the circumstantial evidence was pointing at Lamb, the judge was unconvinced. In his summing up speech to the jury, he made the following points:

> the case rested mainly, if not entirely, on the credit they were disposed to give to Sibley's evidence; for without it there were no facts sufficiently strong to convict the prisoner, though certainly all the facts were consistent with the supposition that the prisoner committed the murder, and none directly contradicted that supposition.

It was observed that Lamb would be unlikely to feel the need to unburden himself to another, as he was a hardened criminal. It was more likely that Sibley saw the chance to free himself from gaol and earn the reward money, now amounting to £220. It all depended, the judge argued, on Sibley's character and motives.

The jury deliberated for a mere half an hour. They decided to give Lamb the benefit of the doubt. He returned to prison, presumably to serve the remaining weeks of his sentence for poaching, but had escaped the gallows.

It seems probable, though not certain, that Lamb was guilty. He was seen walking in the direction of the wood and returned from it some time later. He was a well-known criminal and may have sought revenge for his friends being sent down, partly on the evidence of the lad. On the other hand, there was no direct evidence or witnesses to prove that he was guilty. It is possible that someone else was responsible, perhaps Lavender or Bray. It will remain an unsolved mystery, as will the murder of William Howard in 1816.

CHAPTER 8

A Schoolboy Stabbing in Hayes, 1839

he immediately, with his right hand, made a back handed stab at the deceased, and struck him in the belly.

Violent deaths of schoolboys, usually by stabbing, make dramatic newspaper headlines in the early twenty-first century. Yet, as with much in criminal history, they were not unknown in the past, either, albeit at a lower level. For instance, two pupils at Eton in 1825 had had a boxing match, in which one of the pugilists died. A similar incident, which is about to be related, occurred in Hayes.

The Revd Frederick Sturmer (1804–76) had been educated at Queen's College, Oxford, and had been curate in Hayes since 1835. Like many clergymen, he was also a schoolmaster, running a small, select boys' school there. The school was run from Sturmer's own house in Wood End Green, and in 1839 there were only four young men there. One was Francis Medhurst, aged 21, though he was really a boarder, rather than a pupil. Although born in England, he had spent most of his life, until his late teens, in Italy. His father was dead, but his mother still lived. He was about to become a wealthy man, and was to inherit property which would give him an income of £7,000 per annum. However, his family history was unfortunate. His grandfather murdered his wife in York in 1804, using a knife. Because he was deemed insane, he was committed to a private asylum – Moorcrofts in Hillingdon, run by one Robert Stillwell, in fact. Joseph Alsop, another pupil, had only been with Sturmer for a few weeks, was aged 18 and was also a wealthy young gentleman.

It was the morning of Saturday 9 March 1839. A lesson was about to begin. At 10, Maximilian Dalison, one of Sturmer's pupils, left the house. Medhurst, wearing his dressing gown, entered the room in which Alsop and Edward Baring, another

Queen's College, Oxford, c. 1900. Author's collection

of Sturmer's pupils, were located. Sturmer was also present. Medhurst was carrying a stick and announced to Sturmer, 'See what a blackguard has just left your house. See, he has broken the glass of my watch.' At which Medhurst showed the clergyman his watch, the glass of which had been broken.

Alsop turned around and said to him, 'You are a liar and a blackguard for saying so'. According to Sturmer, Medhurst then attacked Alsop and hit him with his stick and a scuffle broke out. Sturmer chose that moment to leave the room. He later said, 'I left the room because the prisoner [Medhurst] was a gentleman of very hasty temper, and I knew it was no use interfering at that time'. Edward Baring who remained there throughout later recalled:

Medhurst then took a great stick which he had in his hand, and with both hands struck at the deceased's head with it, and the blows either fell on his head or his arms, which were held up to protect it. Deceased then wrenched the stick from Medhurst, and, I believe, struck at him in return. They then separated a distance of about six or eight feet, the deceased retaining the stick. The deceased was then coming up again with the stick to hit Mr Medhurst, and then advanced about four feet when Mr Medhurst put his two hands to his trousers' pocket, on the left side, and drew out a spring knife with an ivory handle ... he immediately, with his right hand, made a back handed stab at the deceased, and struck him in the belly ... Medhurst made a long stride towards him, stooping at the time, and, having stabbed him, drew back and went round a table and out of the room.

Alsop collapsed to the floor, saying 'He has stabbed me'. All this took two minutes. Sturmer returned, to see if he could stop the fight, but by then it was over. Medhurst was leaving the room and Alsop was groaning on the floor. Baring also left the room and then the house, stating: 'I will be a witness'.

Sturmer noticed there was blood on Alsop's clothes, but did not see the wound until the following day. Alsop was taken to his room. Medhurst later went in and Sturmer overheard Alsop say to him, 'We were both wrong; I forgive you.' Meanwhile, Benjamin Chadwick, MRCS, of Hayes, was summoned. He examined Alsop's wounds. The stab wound was on the left side of the body and was about an inch and a half in length and was wide and gaping. Alsop asked 'Is it mortal?' Chadwick reassured him, 'No, it was not'. Thinking

The Lych Gate and Hayes Church, c. 1890. Philip Sherwood's collection

the wound to be superficial, he knit it together and applied plasters and bandages. He thought the wound was only a minor one and told this to Sturmer. Medhurst visited Alsop again and expressed his regret.

Chadwick made another visit that day, arriving at about 4 pm. The patient seemed far more comfortable. Chadwick was all reassurance. He said, 'Let us inquire into your general state of health: were you always a healthy young man?'

Alsop replied, 'Yes, but some years ago I had epileptic fits.' The last had been four years before. Chadwick asked if he had any other ailments or injuries. Alsop told him about his sore head, which had received a knock from Medhurst's stick earlier that day. He also complained about the state of his bowels. Chadwick gave the young man some medicine. He saw him again at 10 to check that Alsop had taken his pills and medicine, which he had, but without enthusiasm.

Sturmer sent an express for Alsop's aunts, who soon arrived and stayed with him for the next few days. Medhurst was taken into custody. On the following morning, Sturmer called for Mr Patten, an Uxbridge surgeon. Chadwick was recalled and they met at the house at ten in the morning. Patten had Alsop stripped of his clothes, washed and had the bandages removed so that he could examine him the better, which Chadwick disapproved of. Patten applied a poultice and 24 leeches. That evening the surgeons returned and removed the leeches. Alsop vomited up the medicine he had been given. More leeches were applied on the Monday and the skin around the wound was looking blue – most unhealthy.

However, when they visited on Tuesday, Alsop seemed better, though the vomiting continued and he was still constipated. The following day saw a rapid deterioration in his condition and Sturmer was of the opinion that he would not recover. Another surgeon, Ralph Frogley, from Hounslow, arrived on this day. He told Patten that 'there was no possibility of his surviving'. Frogley asked Alsop about the fracas with Medhurst. Alsop told him 'I had forgiven Mr Medhurst and can say no more'. Frogley asked if he had provoked the quarrel with Medhurst. Alsop replied, 'I called him a liar and a blackguard, upon which he struck me'. On

Thursday the young man was dead. Chadwick carried out a post mortem on the following day. According to him, the cause of death was:

> From inflammation of the bowels. Extravastion of blood in the cavity of the abdomen with a detention from flatus in the bowels. The cause came from the wound I have described.

The type of weapon used, must have been, according to Chadwick,

> a thin instrument without a back. I would say a sharp, clean, thin double cutting instrument. Both extremities of the wound corresponded externally. I mean a double-edged instrument. The wound had penetrated through the penteoeum, and had entered the omentum or fat lining the bowels.

The inquest took place on the following Saturday, 16 March, in the parlour of Sturmer's house. The jury was made up of seventeen respectable local men, including Chadwick Jones, a barrister. Mr Wakley, MP, presided. Once the jury was sworn in, they went upstairs to view the corpse. Only they, the coroner and the surgeons had seen the body. That gruesome task being over, they went downstairs, but finding the parlour rather too small for comfort, they adjourned, as juries often did, to a nearby inn. This was the Adam and Eve, on the Uxbridge Road, Hayes.

The witnesses were called: Sturmer, the surgeons, Baring. The latter was shown Medhurst's knife, which he identified as having been the fatal weapon. He remembered Medhurst showing it to him before the fight. Baring was asked if there was any prior animosity between Medhurst and Alsop.

Medhurst had quarrelled with Dalison in the week before the murder and had not spoken to him since. It was also revealed that Medhurst owned a brace of pistols and a dagger. Baring had heard him say, 'there is such a thing as a good stab with a knife'. There had been a disagreement between Medhurst and Alsop about the use of a hassock in church, which made

The Adam and Eve, Uxbridge Road, Hayes, 1900. Philip Sherwood's collection

Medhurst aggrieved. Frogley thought it best to say that he had asked Alsop if there was anything premeditated in Medhurst's attack, to which Alsop had answered 'Definitely not'.

Given the length of time which had been spent on the medical evidence, the coroner decided to adjourn the inquest until Monday. All jurors were bound over for £40 to return. One objected, saying that he did not mind sitting up until midnight if that was what it took to complete the inquest. The coroner was not impressed and rebuked him:

> Gentlemen, that will not do. An enquiry of this serious nature ought not to be hurried over in that manner, but ought to be most maturely weighed, as the consequences may be most momentous to one individual. I shall therefore, after I have finished with the evidence of the medical gentlemen, suggest an adjournment.

Next day there was some discussion of the stick used by Medhurst, which could not be located. Baring described it as being made out of vine and had a knob the size of an egg. Baring was then asked about Medhurst's character. He said, 'I dare say there were faults on both sides. We could not agree;

he had such nasty sneaking ways, telling everything.' Sturmer was also asked to comment about this and he said that Medhurst was not generally popular with the younger lads. He added that Alsop had had a quarrel with Medhurst a week before the fatal fray, and that once the others had locked Medhurst out of the bedroom they shared. He also said that Medhurst had an 'Italian' temperament. Dalison also gave evidence, but it was scarcely different to anyone else's. It seems that Medhurst was unpopular with the younger men and they baited him. This may have led to him arming himself, and being quick to resent any slight. It made him dangerous, or rather they had helped make him so.

The coroner told the jury that they had to decide whether this was a case of murder or the lesser one of manslaughter. The distinction, he reminded them, was not an easy one to make. If they believed that Medhurst had meant to slay Alsop, then, of course, it was murder. After nearly an hour's discussion, the seventeen-man jury, with two dissidents, concluded that it was a case of murder by Medhurst. But they also presented another conclusion:

> The jury are unanimously of the opinion that the conduct of Mr Sturmer is highly reprehensible in not interfering to prevent the altercation between the parties, as such interference might have prevented the unhappy consequences which have ensued.

Meanwhile, what of Medhurst himself? He had been given into the charge of Sergeant Cooper, of Uxbridge police station. Initially, on hearing the evidence at the inquest he was calm, leaving everything to his legal representatives. Then his mood changed and he became depressed. He then requested the Bible and the Prayer Book to read in order to console his increasingly troubled mind. After being told of the jury's verdict, he was ordered to be sent to Newgate to await trial. The corpse of Alsop was buried in Tottenham churchyard.

But Medhurst's fate was not to be sent to Newgate immediately. The coroner who had made out that warrant had not acted properly, as he did not have that power, which lay

Moorcroft Asylum, now flats, 2006. Philip Sherwood's collection

with the local magistrates. They needed to examine Medhurst in order to decide whether he should be sent there for trial or not.

This was held in the King's Arms on Uxbridge High Street (which closed in 1960 and is currently used as an employment agency). Medhurst looked pale and worried, as well he might. The watch he said Alsop broke was shown to the court and it was shown to have had a piece of glass missing. Then there was discussion about the medical evidence. It was discussed whether the wound which Alsop received would have been enough to kill him if he were in the best of health, which he may not have been. Yet it was concluded that such an injury would have proved deadly.

Mr Clark, a Hayes churchwarden, recalled a conversation with Medhurst on the day after the fight. Apparently, Medhurst told him, 'It's true I have cut him with a knife. It was in the heat of passion, and I am sorry for it.' Mr Stammers, Medhurst's barrister, argued that the jury should only commit Medhurst on the charge of manslaughter, not murder. He pointed out how solicitous Medhurst had been towards Alsop after he had struck the blow. He also said that the blow had not been planned in advance, quoting previous case history to show that malice must be proved for a crime to

The King's Arms (now an employment agency), 2007. Author's collection

be constituted as murder. In conclusion, 'the whole chain of the evidence proved the prisoner was not actuated by malice towards the deceased, but at the impulse of the moment, pulled out the knife and stabbed him'. Despite this, Medhurst was judged to be charged on the crime of murder. The tearful youth bowed to the court once he knew the next stage of the drama.

The trial at the Old Bailey took place on the morning of Saturday 13 April. The courtroom was packed with spectators, so that 'several ladies who contrived to squeeze into court were obliged to remain standing during the whole of the trial. The multiplication of wigs and gowns was truly marvellous.' Medhurst was allowed to sit during the whole proceeding. He was dressed in black and looked dejected.

The prosecution outlined the case against him, and yet again Sturmer was reprimanded for not having interposed his authority to prevent the fight. Baring gave his version of the events leading up to the fight, as well as the encounter itself. Sturmer was called forth to do likewise. He added that he knew Medhurst had a knife; the latter had told Sturmer this was because of his interest in carpentry and, indeed, he had had materials brought down to him from Uxbridge for that purpose. He also said that Medhurst valued the watch highly because it had belonged to his late father, who had died in 1837. Chadwick gave medical evidence.

The argument was put that Medhurst was only defending himself, and that Alsop was a taller and more powerful youth, though younger by three years. It was regrettable that a knife had been used 'and it was equally to be lamented that the practice of carrying such weapons had lately sprang up in this country'. The defence barrister wished that a law could be passed to make the sale of such lethal weapons illegal. Other witnesses testified to Medhurst's good character and humanity.

After summing up the evidence, the jury retired and took half an hour to find the prisoner guilty of manslaughter. The judge said that he hoped Medhurst would spend the next few years 'in a sincere attempt to regulate your temper by recalling to your mind the proceedings of this day, and that by a sincere repentance for that great crime you have committed'. Had Sturmer 'done his duty, as a man, as a tutor and as a clergyman, instead of leaving the room as he did, the fearful catastrophe would have been prevented'. Medhurst was sentenced to three years in the House of Correction in Coldbath Fields, London.

None of the central protagonists of the drama came out well. Alsop was dead, Medhurst in prison, though at least still alive, and Sturmer's reputation had collapsed by his one moment of inaction. However, by 1845 he may have put it down to a mere local difficulty, as he was appointed Rector of Heapham in Lincolnshire.

CHAPTER 9

The Second Stabbing in 1839

… it was with deep regret that the offence of stabbing was on the increase in this country.

The year 1839 was a grim one for sudden death in this locality, at least by nineteenth-century standards, if not our own. Both concerned young lads. Another contemporary touch was the judge's comments.

Central to the bloody drama was one George Coker, described as 'a mild-looking youth, aged 15' and 'a quiet and in offensive boy'. Three accounts were given of the fatal affray, which occurred at Harefield at about 9.30 pm on Saturday 3 August 1839. According to Benjamin Somerville, a Harefield baker, Moses Gates, aged 21 or 22, and much bigger than Coker, was standing by his fish stall in Harefield. Somerville was only a few yards away. The first he knew of any trouble was when he turned to see Gates hit Coker twice. Gates told Coker he would not cut salmon for him unless he meant to pay for it.

Coker briefly quitted the scene, then returned and exchanged words with Gates, and these were not heard by Somerville. Gates ran towards Coker, then retreated to his stall. Coker then threatened him, telling him if he attacked him again, he would not run away another time, but would fight back. There was another fracas, and Gates said he had been stabbed. Somerville saw blood on his trousers. More blood was flowing from a wound in his stomach.

The second witness was Edward Clift, who said that Gates was weighing his pickled salmon when Coker came up to him and asked, 'Who is to give you a penny an ounce for your salmon?' Gates was not amused and retorted, 'Who is going to weigh salmon for you when you won't take it after it is weighed?' He then hit Coker on the face. Coker said, 'You b–, if you hit me again, you shall have something for it; I shan't run'. He repeated these words at least once more.

Under such provocation, Gates attacked him again. Coker ran down the road, followed by Gates. Coker had been waving his arms about. He then stopped and rushed towards his pursuer, crying, 'Now you have got it!' Gates clutched his stomach and, returning to his stall, declared, 'He has stabbed me with a dagger'.

Nathaniel Hattstead was the final witness. He thought that Gates hit Coker twice or thrice on the first occasion. Coker had hid behind Hattstead at one point, and was in tears. He then said something about striking him and Gates went for him a second time. Gates struck him another three times, making five or six blows in all, before he was stabbed. The whole incident lasted about five minutes. Finally, William Parr, a lad, said that Coker had done all he could do to escape Gates.

Shortly afterwards, Mr Bullock, a surgeon was called for. But he did not see Gates until 3 am the following day. He examined the wound which he saw as being dangerous. He applied what remedies he could, but such was the loss of blood that Gates died just after midnight on 4 August.

Later on the night of the affray, one John Atkins, the parish constable, visited Coker, who was in bed at his father's house. Atkins took the boy's knife from his trouser pocket. It was a common clasp knife 'such as boys usually carry'. It was also bloodstained. Although Coker denied it was blood, he said that he was not sorry for what he had done, because he had been struck first. Atkins gave the knife to Charles Murray, head constable of the parish. Coker was taken by Atkins to Newgate on 7 August, after the inquest had been held.

There was debate over what offence Coker should be tried for. The coroner believed it should be murder, but the magistrates who examined the case believed it should be manslaughter. The case came before the Old Bailey on 15 August. The three main witnesses' evidence was given, as outlined above. Atkins displayed the knife and Bullock told what he knew. However, Parr was not present and it was only through the good offices of the prosecution that his statement

Harefield, c. *1900.* Author's collection

could be read out in court at all. In fact, the defence made much of the coroner overruling the magistrates in making the trial one of murder, not manslaughter. The coroner's action was termed 'most mischievous and unprecedented'. The defence argued that this should not even be a case of manslaughter, but one of self defence, by a smaller lad against a larger one, and then only after the former had tried to run away. He appealed to the jury to show mercy.

Mr Justice Williams did not feel able to comment about the dispute between the coroner and the magistrates which the defence had emphasized, but said that it was usual, in cases of this kind, that the more serious charge be preferred. In any case, the jury acquitted Coker of murder, but found him guilty of manslaughter. It is worth quoting Williams at this point:

He could not sufficiently deprecate the un-English and unmanly practice of resorting to the use of a knife in a sudden quarrel, and it was with deep regret that the offence of stabbing was on the increase in this country. It became the bounden duty, therefore, both of judges and magistrates, to quell as disgraceful a practice as far as the law could so.

Because of this, an example had to be shown. Coker was transported to Australia for the rest of his life. On hearing the verdict, the lad fainted. He was sent to Van Diemen's Land (now known as Tasmania) on board the *Runnymede* on 11 November 1839. In an earlier decade he might have been hanged.

On the following day, there was a letter in *The Times*, commenting on the verdicts in the case of Medhurst and that of Coker: 'On reading the account of the trial of George Coker, for murder, I was struck with the analogy between this case and that of Medhurst'. It will be recalled that Medhurst was 21 years old and educated, and Coker was but 15 and uneducated. Furthermore, Medhurst had been the aggressor and Coker had been the aggrieved party. Yet Coker was transported for life and Medhurst was to serve only three years in prison.

It is possible that there was some earlier antagonism between the two principals in the conflict, but we do not know what it was. If not, the regrettable fact is that Coker had a lethal weapon and in the heat of the moment, he used it.

CHAPTER 10

Murder in Uxbridge, 1869

*… the sudden excess of bloodthirsty passion, the
inspiration of drunkenness.*

he Buckinghamshire Advertiser showed its horror at
this crime in no uncertain fashion, beginning its
reportage of it thus:

A fearful crime – unprecedented, so far as we can learn, in
the modern history of this locality – was perpetrated at the
town of Uxbridge early on the evening of Tuesday last – the
crime of murder, most deliberately accomplished, and as –
it would seem – from no imaginable motive, and no
intelligible cause, except from the sudden excess of
bloodthirsty passion, the inspiration of drunkenness.

It was fortunate that the writer did not live to see subsequent
ages.

The two principal characters in the drama were William
Murray and Frederick Redrup. The latter was 'a harmless and
inoffensive young man', aged 32, and known locally as Tom.
He was simple, but good natured and had no regular
employment. He helped his father in selling and delivering
newspapers and lived with his parents opposite the Market
House. His father had carried on that business, together with
barbering, for many years and was thought most respectable.

William Murray was a younger man, aged 23. His father had
been a gardener, but had died a few years before, by falling
from a tree at Belmont. His son was a bricklayer's labourer and
lived in Smith's Buildings on Rockingham Road. This was
near to the church school, where his widowed mother worked.
Murray was not vicious, but he did have one vice – drink. He
was described as 'greatly addicted to drink, and has been in

Uxbridge High Street, c. 1900. Author's collection

the oft habit of coming home, especially for some months past, sometimes two or three times a day, in a drunken state: and when in that condition, he has been lately known to utter threats of being revenged'.

Redrup had been at Denham on the morning of the fatal day – Tuesday 6 July 1869. He returned home for his dinner and drank a half pint of beer. He left home at about 4, perfectly sober. Murray had not been at work that morning. However, though his working pattern was inconsistent, on that day he had some spare money. On taking a recruit to enlist at the barracks, he had been given 5 shillings. Murray met Redrup and they began a drinking spree.

They left the Railway Hotel (opposite the railway station and demolished in 1980), Uxbridge High Street, at about 6. A quarter of an hour later, the young men were arm in arm and walking towards Murray's home. Although inebriated, they seemed on the best of terms. They went into the building. Ann Gowlett, a neighbour, followed them, a few minutes later.

Redrup was lying on the floor and Murray was sitting next to him. Murray stated that they came in 'to take a dram' together. Murray's married sister soon arrived and he explained that 'he had brought Tom in because they would not put upon him'. Redrup thanked them for their concern.

Murray lay down too, as if to sleep off the alcohol. A cushion was put under Redrup's head. The two women then left the room.

Ten minutes later, Murray was seen leaving the building. His sister thought this was odd and went to investigate. The door was shut – she pulled it open and a shock awaited her eyes. Redrup lay in a pool of blood. The young woman shrieked. This attracted the neighbours. Their initial impression was that Redrup had ruptured a blood vessel, so one of them ran to find a doctor. However:

> a closer inspection revealed the dreadful fact that the throat was cut from ear to ear, the head being almost severed. A razor lay open on a chair about three feet off, and the place was deluged with blood. Life was almost extinct. The poor creature was observed to breathe a few times, and then vitality ceased. No struggle had taken place – not a word had been heard. The deed was done as quickly and deliberately as effectually; and the murderer, having gratified his fiendish appetite for blood, had washed his hands in a basin, in which

The Market Place, Uxbridge, 2007. Author's collection

the discoloured water still remained, and wiped them with a cloth which was stained with blood and went out as if nothing had happened.

Murray went to the Market Place and told those there what he had done. John Vagg, a butcher of Windsor Street, was among the audience, and he went in search of PC James West, who took Murray into charge. Although Murray had been drinking, he seemed aware of his words and actions. The policeman went to the scene of the crime to check that the violent deed had actually been done. Dr John Spencer Ferris, who examined the body at about 7.05, noted that the fatal blow had severed the windpipe and the principal arteries. Even had there been instant medical aid at hand, it would have been useless. A razor lay nearby. On it was scratched the word 'Murray'.

PC West told Murray, 'Consider yourself in my custody on a charge of wilful murder of Frederick Redrup. Be careful what you say.' Whilst Murray was being taken to the station house, he saw an acquaintance of his, one William Hay. Murray shook Hay's hand and said 'Come on and have a pot of beer, for I will never see you again.' Hay declined. Murray would not say why he committed the crime and no one could guess. As news of the murder spread, many locals gathered to see where it had occurred.

This event was one of great importance. The local newspaper observed:

The oldest inhabitants state that they never remember to have seen the town as much excited. Consternation and horror were everywhere depicted. The crime was so apparently purposeless, that conjecture was entirely at fault, and people could only conclude that the wretched criminal was frenzied with drink: and that his madness took the homicidal form which that dreadful malady when brought on by intemperance, is sometimes known to assume.

On the following day the prisoner was taken, handcuffed, to the town hall, where the magistrates met at noon. As expected, there was a large crowd. The clerk to the court read the charge against Murray, who seemed perfectly calm, even indifferent. A number of witnesses were then called.

George Redrup, a 32-year-old printer, and the deceased's brother, was the first to be called. He had last seen his brother on Monday, and heard about his death at 7 on the following evening. He said that he had noticed a bloodstained razor on the chair in the room where his brother had been found, and remarked that he thought it belonged to the accused. He added that his brother and Murray were on friendly terms, but not overly so. He recalled seeing Murray at the police station and Murray had said to him 'You know nothing about it: you were not there; if you had been, you would have been in the same position as he is now.'

Vagg was then asked to speak. He recalled that on the previous evening he had heard Murray tell William Nicholls that he had killed Redrup with a razor. Others heard this conversation too, and then Vagg went for the police. Vagg said that Murray had told him and Redrup's father that 'I have cut the b–'s throat, and I meant to have another, but had not the chance'. George Redrup thought that the remark might have been intended to relate to Murray's sister, who was also present. Vagg remembered seeing bloodstains on Murray's trousers and asked how they had got there. Murray replied, 'I helped kill a bullock last week', but Vagg thought that the stains were too fresh for that to be true.

Ferris was called upon to give the medical evidence. He said that there were two cuts; one oblique and one straight. They could not have been self-inflicted. There was also blood on the victim's hands, and to each side of his body. The furniture nearby had been untouched.

George Ilbery, a baker and neighbour, recalled being asked by others to enter the room, which he did just before 7, and saw the corpse. Robert Carter recalled seeing the two men between 6 and 7 and that Murray had great difficulty in moving Redrup, who was lying on the ground. Carter had offered to help, but Murray refused this aid, saying, 'Let him come down to my house. If you do not like to help him down, let him alone.'

Other witnesses testified to seeing the two men enter the building. Ann Gowlett recalled some words of Murray's which he said over a week before the murder. Murray had been eating and then went to fetch an instrument, which he took to the doorway, and began to sharpen. He said 'I have sharpened this, for I mean to have my bloody revenge.'

At this point, the clerk of the court asked Murray if he had anything to say on the matter. Murray replied, 'I have nothing to say.' The chairman of the court concluded that there was enough evidence to commit Murray for trial for murder. The court would reconvene on the following day, after the inquest, in order to consider any additional evidence. The hall cleared and Murray was escorted to prison at Clerkenwell.

The inquest was held at the Chequers Hotel, Uxbridge High Street (demolished in 1961) on the following morning. As it was Saturday, and thus market day in Uxbridge, the court was packed with onlookers. The jury were obliged to view Redrup's corpse first of all. Much the same evidence was given here as had already been given the previous day by the likes of George Redrup, John Vagg and Dr Ferris.

Murray was allowed to speak. He pleaded 'not guilty' on the grounds that he had been drunk at the time of the murder. He had nothing more to say, but some thought he had a callous air about him. He was told he would be put on trial at the Old Bailey at the next sessions. Locals concluded that Murray was harmless enough when sober, but not when drunk, and that his behaviour may have been getting worse because he had been disappointed in love, having been jilted by a girl. This caused his recent behaviour to become increasingly eccentric. He had been seen precariously balancing himself on the window ledge in the building he lived, so some thought he might kill himself by falling. No one could guess why he would kill Redrup, except on some sudden impulse. He had been in trouble with the police, however, not only for drunkenness, but also for assault. It was even rumoured that he had taken part in a burglary.

The trial took place on 15 July. Ann Gowlett was the principal witness, testifying to Murray's sharpening his knife and issuing a vague threat. She also reported seeing the two men together shortly before the murder. Other witnesses testified as before. Dr Ferris was asked to elaborate about the effect of drink. He said;

Habitual drunkenness would produce a diseased state of the brain – an inflammatory condition. Frenzy, perhaps, would be a better term, and persons in that condition often lapse into a state of delirium tremens, when they lost control over their actions. If the prisoner had received a severe blow on the head about six weeks before, that would render him more open to the influence of drink.

Mr Ribton, defending, said that the accused and the victim had been on the best of terms, and no one had heard them quarrel. They were both drunk. Therefore, there could be no 'malice aforethought'. Although drunkenness could not be used to excuse the crime, it was of great importance when it came to the question of intention. Thus there were extenuating circumstances. Murray had borne no malice towards Redrup. There was no motive or prior intent to kill.

Justice Bovill told the jury that voluntary drunkenness was no defence for a criminal. It did not reduce the crime of murder to one of manslaughter. Otherwise, there would be no defence against crimes committed by those who were drunk. Although malice aforethought was necessary to prove murder, if one man took another's life then malice was presumed. He told the jury to dismiss Murray's threat made while sharpening his knife, but that they should decide whether they were absolutely certain that it was Murray's hand which used the razor to kill the unfortunate Redrup. There was no insanity in the case and drink was no excuse for murder.

The jury did not need to leave the court and made up their minds within ten minutes. They found Murray guilty of murder. The judge donned his black cap and duly passed the death sentence. He said that everything had been done for the accused, but he had been found guilty on the evidence offered. He remarked 'It was another lamentable instance of the habits of intemperance, which was sapping the foundations of virtue and comfort among the working classes'. Murray bore the verdict with much fortitude, even smiling when he heard it. He was less affected by it than anyone in the court. Yet he was not hanged, but sent to prison, where he died in 1879.

Why Murray committed the murder is still unclear. He was probably feeling angry and in drink was often violent. Redrup had the great misfortune to be in the wrong place at the wrong time. Murray might have killed anyone.

CHAPTER 11

A Family Butcher, 1870

There is a man near Uxbridge who owes me some money, and if I don't get it off him next time I go, I'll murder him.

Although this most savage event took place just to the north of Uxbridge, it has been included because of the magnitude of the offence, which may be unique in British criminal history. Part of the drama was played out in Uxbridge in any case.

Emmanuel Marshall, aged about 35, lived in a cottage adjacent to his smithy, not far from the Oxford High Road, near Denham. With him was his wife, Charlotte, 34. They had four children: Mary, aged 8, Thereasa, 6, and Gertrude 4, and Francis William, who was a baby and had been sent to briefly stay with relatives. This was because Marshall's sister, Mary Ann, aged 30, was staying with them as she was to be wed on 24 May. George Amor of Herefordshire was her fiancé and had known her for four years; the engagement had been a long one. Finally, there was Mary, aged 77 and Marshall's mother. The cottage was roomy and Marshall was known to be an industrious man. To all intents and purposes, they seemed contented and comfortably off. On Saturday 20 May, the two elder children were seen playing in the road. Little did they know that sudden and swift destruction was about to be their lot.

It was on the evening of Monday 22 May 1870 that the shocking discovery was made. This was either by someone who was delivering a wedding dress, or by labourers who needed Marshall to do some work for them. PC Charles Taverner, based in Denham, was the first policeman on the scene, having been alerted by a young man from the village. He later told the magistrates at the inquest the shocking news:

I went to the house and found the doors open. I found two bodies – the wife and the sister – lying just inside the door, and the sister's feet towards her head. A petticoat covered them. About two feet from them was a sledge hammer ... This was covered with blood. I then went into the washhouse and found the bodies of the three children. I found an axe ... also covered with blood ... There were extensive wounds on the heads of all the bodies ... I found the body of Emmanuel, the father, in the forge, a house adjoining, lying flat on his face, with his hands stretched out.

Mary Marshall's dead body was also found. All the corpses were dressed in their night clothes only. A poker was found near the corpses and it had been used on them, as well as the axe and the sledge hammer.

The constable went upstairs. All three of the beds had been slept in. He could find no evidence of any struggle. He thought that the people had hastily left their beds and run out of their rooms. Marshall had his working clothes on, but not his boots. Another set of clothes was found in the cottage. Taverner described these thus:

There is blood on these clothes. There were a pair of boots, trousers, a coat, a cord jacket. A cord vest, a slop, a deerstalker's hat, and a red and white common plaid neckcloth.

Taverner explained that he had seen a man dressed in these clothes at about 3 am on Sunday. He had been on patrol and he had met a man who had the look of the mechanic about him and had been shabbily dressed. This man told Taverner that he had seen a man threatening to throw his wife into the nearby canal. The man who Taverner met explained that he was a stranger in the district and asked for directions, setting off in the direction of the Marshalls' house.

This mysterious man was next seen at about 7 am, though he was mistaken by the witness, one Elizabeth Simpson, as being Marshall himself, as he was attired in Marshall's Sunday clothing and was seen coming from his house. He was carrying

Denham village, c. *1900.* Author's collection

a carpet bag with him (this had not been seen by Taverner a few hours previously). She was looking for a missing key and he travelled with her for some time, telling her the same story about a man threatening his wife. When Elizabeth told him of her thinking he was Marshall, he replied that the family had left the house at about 5 for a holiday.

Later that morning, John Smith, a coal dealer of Denham, who was sitting outside his cottage, was approached by the stranger. He offered to sell him a watch, but he declined the sale, as he already had one. It was now about 7.55. He then offered to buy Smith a drink in Uxbridge, to which the latter consented.

Finally, the mysterious man came to the Dog and Duck pub at about 8. Sarah Aldeman was the publican. She recalled that he asked for a pint of beer. She said that she did not serve until half past noon, and he retorted that he had travelled from Wycombe and so claimed travellers' rights to refreshment. He had his beer and paid a shilling for it. He was carrying a carpet bag. She thought that his attire was like that of Marshall's. Although the man seemed exhausted, he only stayed about ten minutes and did not finish his drink.

Superintendent Dunham of the Buckinghamshire Police arrived later that evening to take charge. He noticed that Charlotte and her sister-in-law were only in their nightdresses, though the latter had her boots on. Their nightdresses were torn, indicating that they had been dragged to their present place after being killed elsewhere. The bodies of these two women were found close together. The corpses of the elder children were in the back kitchen. The elder Mrs Marshall was partially dressed and beside her lay the youngest child, dressed only in a chemise. Marshall's body had been dragged around the forge, as his face was 'as black as a coal', due to the ash on the floor. Two drawers of a bureau had been opened and a watch case was found to be empty.

On the following day, the police began a major manhunt. Every alehouse, lodging house and public house in the vicinity of Brentford and Uxbridge was visited. Officials were also sent down from Scotland Yard to help. One suspect was a man who had been committed to prison for two months in the previous year, on the strength of Marshall's evidence. Yet the solution was near at hand and a lucky break led them to the killer.

As said, the massacre was not discovered until the evening of Monday 22 May but news quickly spread. Charles Coombes, a bricklayer of Uxbridge, who resided at Mrs Ballam's lodging house at Bell Yard, had heard the news whilst in the Queen's Arms on that night. He was with another man when the news was announced. The latter then asked Coombes to show him out of the pub by the back door. Coombes returned to hear the news and his friend reappeared ten minutes later. Coombes then went off to bed, as he had to be at work by 6 on the following morning. Coombes recalled that the man had asked him to buy a silver watch earlier that day, which he had declined. The man pawned it and seemed flush with money, treating Coombes to beer and spending lavishly on a couple of women he accompanied on Sunday and Monday.

On the following morning he became very suspicious of this acquaintance of his, and he told his employer about this. Coombes then reported the matter to the police. The desk sergeant showed Coombes the clothes found at the Marshall house which were probably those of the killer. He had seen these on his acquaintance, who he had met on Saturday afternoon (20 May). He had previously known the man, who he called Jack, but whose real name was John Owen (aged 38) and for sake of simplicity I shall subsequently refer to him by this name. He had been sent to prison earlier that year for thefts committed after he had left his lodgings at night times. Owen now had no carpet bag and no money. He declined Coombes's offer to go to the pub that evening. Owen had left the lodgings he shared with Coombes on the Saturday night and had not returned until about 10 am the following day. Coombes related: 'He was then attired quite differently from what he had on when he first took the lodgings.' Coombes told his acquaintance, 'Why, I don't know you again, hardly.' Owen explained that he had visited his brother's house and the latter had supplied him with a new set of clothes. When the landlady heard this, she said, 'There is something done wrong by that fellow, for it don't stand to reason that a brother would strip himself of clothes and a watch.'

Coombes related how Owen had told him that he was going to Reading. It was 5 on Tuesday morning and he came into Coombes's bedroom, and said, 'Have you any bacca [tobacco]?' Coombes had not, and then was asked if he had any breakfast. Coombes had little, but said he would happily share what he had. Owen then announced he was going for the 6.45 train to Reading. This turned out to be a fatal mistake.

That afternoon, Coombes went to Reading by train. He was met at Slough by Superintendent Dunham, and at Reading. PC Toulman joined them. At Reading, they searched numerous lodging houses until they found the Oxford Arms, otherwise known as the Tramp's Kitchen, in Silver Street. Dunham later said, 'I went into the kitchen, which was behind the house, and there were about a dozen men and women there. Coombes at once said, pointing ... "That's the man"'.

Owen then said, 'I never murdered man, woman, or child', though he later denied saying these incriminating words. Dunham recalled:

I crossed over to him at once and seized him by the throat. The Reading policeman who was with me – Toulman is his name – said, 'Mind, he's pulling something out of his pocket!' and, crossing over, I seized his arm, and took hold of the pistol which the prisoner took from his pocket.

The pistol was loaded up to the muzzle with powder, slugs and a piece of iron wire. Dunham remarked, 'You are charged with murdering seven people, among them Emmanuel Marshall' and put handcuffs on him. His prisoner replied, 'I have not murdered anyone, but I know who did.' Dunham said, 'You have the murdered man's boots and some of his clothes on.' Owen replied, 'That may be.'

He was described thus:

> He has a determined looking countenance, and apparently speaks with a Scotch accent. He is about five foot seven high, of sallow complexion, and has a dark beard cut short all round, dark eyes, brown hair and moustache. He was dressed in a kind of printer's cap, clean white smock and dark striped trousers.

Once captured, he was searched. On him was an Uxbridge pawnbroker's ticket for a silver watch with a gold chain that was missing from Marshall's house. He had also pawned the waistcoat and coat that had belonged to the dead man, at a pawnbroker's in Union Street, Reading, for 4 shillings. A small amount of money (5 shillings 6 pence) was also found on his person. Dunham went to the pawnbroker's shop and received the black cloth coat and the waistcoat so recently deposited there. The woman at the shop identified the prisoner as having pawned them. Mr Butcher, the Uxbridge pawnbroker, also identified Owen as having brought the watch to him.

Owen was taken to Reading police station and was escorted onto a train to Slough that evening. Mr Boyce, the Deputy Governor of Reading Gaol, was called for, and he identified the prisoner as a former inmate of the county gaol. He had stolen a barrow from Reading cemetery about eight or ten years before, and more recently had been convicted of stealing a lamb in Abingdon, and was sentenced to eighteen months imprisonment with hard labour (sadly, gone were the days when such an offence could lead to hanging), being released on 8 January 1870. He was then known as John Jones and had, on his last spell at Reading gaol, told the warders he would never spend that amount of time in there again.

The departure of the escort party was watched with interest by over 1,000 people. They bore the prisoner much ill will and hissed at him. Captain Drake, Chief Constable of Buckinghamshire, helped Dunham escort the man onto the train, and they left Reading at 8.10.

On Wednesday 25 May, Owen was examined by the magistrates at the Slough police station. He was variously named as John Jones and John Jennings. He was said to have been once a boilermaker of Staffordshire or a blacksmith of Birmingham, and a widower. Yet he was well known to the suburban police as a tramp and a thief. Crowds surrounded the building and some peered through the windows to catch a glimpse of such a notorious character. When he was brought in, there were loud exclamations by these onlookers. Apparently,

> The man, seen anywhere and under any circumstances would be judged to be a particularly brutal type, his head indicating a thoroughly animal organisation. As seen in the dock, the peculiarly unprepossessing characteristics of the man, were, perhaps, heightened by the circumstances which surrounded him.

He was handcuffed and appeared cool, though when confronted with the clothes he had worn during the murders, still stained with blood and brain, the colour drained from his face.

Dunham told the court about his discovery on Monday evening and then Coombes gave his evidence. He said, 'I can swear to the cap (which is a peculiar one) and to the corduroy jacket. I should not like to swear to the boots. The prisoner wore that cap, which I noticed particularly, as it has a narrow brim, and the jacket on Saturday.' He related all of his evidence, and Owen said that he met Coombes at 5 on Saturday, not 3 as Coombes suggested. The latter admitted he was uncertain about the time of their meeting.

The prisoner was remanded until the following week. He did not seem the least dispirited and replied 'All right' and bid his former acquaintance farewell. The police took him to

Aylesbury Gaol. Again, the mob's anger was all too evident, but the police guarded their prisoner well and he was put on the train.

The police theory was that Owen arrived at the Marshall house when all the family were asleep. He had then awakened Marshall by breaking into the smithy, looking for weapons. When Marshall hastily dressed and went to the smithy, the intruder killed him with a sledge hammer. The man's wife had followed her husband downstairs to see what the matter was. She was then struck down on the threshold of the house. The rest of the family came down in their turn and were likewise killed. The cottage was then plundered. It was thought that the intruder claimed that Marshall owed him money and if he was not paid, he would kill him.

On the day after the hearing, 26 May, there was a funeral service held at Denham's pretty parish church. All the victims, save the elder Mrs Marshall, were buried there. She was not a native of the parish and was conveyed to be buried where she had usually resided. A large stone now marks their grave in the churchyard. The funerals were all the more poignant because of the marriage that had been intended for that week.

Gravestone of the Marshall family in Denham churchyard, 2007. Author's collection

The judicial inquiry proceeded relentlessly; with the coroner's proceedings being resumed and concluded on 27 May. Dunham repeated his tale as to how the accused man was located. However, it was John Ferris, an Uxbridge doctor who had performed the inquest on Redrup the previous year, who gave much of the evidence, chiefly about how the seven victims died. He had been summoned on the Monday evening when the corpses had been found. Three other doctors assisted in his task. According to Ferris, the murders occurred at about 3 am on Sunday. He then went into detail about each body.

After noting some grazes on Marshall's fingers, suggesting that he had tried to defend himself from the attacker, Ferris said:

There were on the face four wounds, one over the right eye, one over the nose, one over the left eye, and a deep one on the chin. The upper and lower jaws, even to the bone under the eye, were completely smashed in. On the head, the hair was matted with blood, and ashes were on it, and on the scalp were five wounds, one on the left side of the head, one behind it, an inch and a half long, another small one behind that, on the back of the head, a large one, on the right side a long lacerated wound. The skull was not fractured by one of these. There was a fracture on the base of the skull from right to left, to such an extent that the skull could be pulled in half. The scalp wounds were probably produced by a poker, and the smashing of the face and fractures by a sledgehammer or the back of an axe.

The description of the wounds suffered by the rest of the family were equally distressing. Ferris then spoke about the 6-year-old Theresea:

On her there was no fracture or bruise of limbs or body, but there was a wound on the scalp and protrusion of brain, and blood was oozing from the right ear, behind which was a small cut. The face was uninjured. On removing the scalp an open face to the brain, of five inches by four inches, was disclosed – a fact the whole right side of the skull was smashed, to the right side of the spine. The whole injuries on the child were produced probably by one blow of the sledge hammer.

Ferris then discussed the 8-year-old Mary:

[She] had no bruise or fracture on body or limbs, but on the head was a semi-circular wound five inches in length, which almost completely cut off the right ear, a small wound above the right ear, other wounds on the back of the head, and near them a 'starred' cut. Three of these were made by a poker, but the starred cut could not have been produced by any instrument yet found. There was a wound on the right side of the face, and both jaws were broken. Inside the skull there was a punctured wound corresponding with the starred cut on the outside, and the base of the skull was fractured across, dividing the skull in half.

Next was the 4-year-old Gertrude:

[She] had blood coming from nose, mouth, and ears, but she had no injuries whatever to body or limbs. All the bones on the left side of the head were completely smashed in – the temple bone alone being intact. Many fragments of bone were detached and there was much blood on the brain. All the injuries to the body were probably done by a sledge hammer.

Mary Ann Marshall was next to be described:

no injury was on the body or limb. There was a slight cut on the upper lip, a wound an inch in length outside the left eye, the teeth of the upper jaw were knocked into a her mouth, a wound an inch and a quarter long was down the parting of the hair, a wound three inches long was on the right side of the head, and these appeared as if done by a sharp axe. There was a large quantity of blood between the brain and the skull, and inside a large amount of blood again, and a fracture at base so great that the skull could be pulled in half. Several pieces of bones were detached.

The injuries of Charlotte, Marshall's wife, were next to be described:

> no injuries were done to body or limbs. On the face the left eyelid was bruised, and there was blood oozing from the left ear. There was a jagged transverse wound an inch long over the right ear, a wound three inches long at back of the head, much blood under the scalp, and a fracture at the base if the skull right across, so the skull could be pulled in half. The injuries were done by a sledge hammer or the back of an axe.

Ferris's professional fellows said that they concurred with him in his assessment of the wounds and how they had been caused. Coombes elaborated on his evidence. Mary Sparks, sister of Marshall's wife, identified Owen's costume as one that her late sister's husband had once owned. A final piece of evidence was that a key had been found at the place where Jones had been arrested. It fitted the lock of the front door of the Marshall house.

The jury concluded that this was a case of wilful murder and Owen was responsible. He would stand trial on the capital charge before the Buckinghamshire assizes at Aylesbury in July.

Public curiosity in the case ran high. On the Sunday following the murder, the Marshalls' house became a popular destination for tourists. Despite being guarded by the police, souvenir hunters descended on the cottage and took what they could. Buses and other forms of transport were labelled 'To Uxbridge, to Denham' in order to cater for the demand. Traffic jams were created by the amount of horse-drawn traffic around Denham and Uxbridge.

At the parish church there were different responses to the dreadful murders. The Revd Charles Joyce, Curate, recalled that only the previous Sunday he had been reading the banns of marriage for the third time – at the same time that the bride to be was lying murdered. Instead of a merry peal of wedding

BENEATH THIS STONE LIE THE REMAINS OF
EMANUEL MARSHALL, AND CHARLOTTE, HIS WIFE,
ALSO MARY ANN, HIS SISTER,
AND MARY, THIRZA AND GERTRUDE HIS CHILDREN,
WHO TOGETHER WITH HIS MOTHER MARY MARSHALL,
WERE ALL BARBAROUSLY MURDERED ON SUNDAY MORNING MAY 22ND 1870
BY JOHN OWENS, A TRAVELLING BLACKSMITH,
WHO WAS EXECUTED IN THE COUNTY GAOL AT AYLESBURY
AUGUST 8TH 1870

MARY AGED 8 YEARS | EMANUEL AGED 35 YEARS | MARY ANN AGED 32 YEARS
THIRZA AGED 6 YEARS | CHARLOTTE AGED 34 YEARS | GERTRUDE AGED 4 YEARS

Gravestone of the Marshall family at Denham churchyard, 2007. Author's collection

bells, there had been the mournful sound of the funeral toll. Apparently, 'During the whole of the sermon scarcely a dry eye could be seen, everyone present being deeply overcome by the excellent sermon delivered.'

There was a further examination of Owen on 30 May. A final piece in the story was now revealed. At 9 am on Saturday 20 May, Owen had been released from Coldbath Fields prison in south London (he had spent two months there for stealing shirts in Uxbridge). He had tramped from there westwards. Henry Salter, a carter, who was employed by an Uxbridge miller, was returning to Uxbridge along the Uxbridge Road on his horse and cart. He met Owen at Hanwell Bridge, where Owen asked if he could have a lift to Uxbridge. Sadler consented. En route, Owen told him he was penniless, but would get some money from his brother at his destination. He alighted at the Green Man, just outside Uxbridge proper, at about 5.30. Salter identified the clothes which Owen wore as being the same as those found in the Marshalls' house. It also emerged that day that the gun that Owen had was owned by Marshall, and that it had been charged at a blacksmith's in Uxbridge on the following day.

The Queen's Head, Windsor Road, Uxbridge, 2007. Author's collection

Baron Channell, in his address to the Grand Jury at Aylesbury on 21 July, announced, 'there is one crime of great magnitude, which will require your attention, but which I think will not make any considerable demand on your time'. He then summarized the case. It was not, however, until the following day that the trial took place, with one Dr Abdy defending Owen.

The case was summarized by the prosecution on 22 July, outlining the discovery of the bodies, and then the witnesses spoke about having seen Owen in Marshall's clothes and going from being penniless to being flush with money on the day of the murder. Goods stolen from the Marshalls had been pawned by Owen – witnesses from Uxbridge and Reading testifying to this.

Abdy, in defending Owen, had an unenviable job, but he did his best. He told the jury to try and forget all they had been told about Owen hitherto. He made four points which he claimed showed the weaknesses in the prosecution's case. First, Abdy said that there was no real evidence linking Owen to the scene of the crime at the time of its having taken place. The only witness to having seen Owen leave the cottage was Mrs Simpson, and it was alleged she was an uncertain witness. Next, he said that the evidence linking Owen to the clues of the clothes were not as strong as the prosecution believed. Finally, Owen appeared calm and collected, which would be improbable for a man guilty of seven murders and on trial for his life.

However, despite this defence, the jury found Owen to be guilty. According to *The Times*,

> He [Owen] listened to the sentence unflinchingly, saying with a military salute, 'Thank you, Sir', and was removed amid the hisses of the audience. At the end of the case the learned Judge called for and passed a high eulogium on Superintendent Dunham, directing that the authorities of the county to give him a reward of £10.

In the weeks between the death sentence being passed on Owen and his execution, fresh facts came to light which illuminated the motive for these most barbarous murders. In 1867, Owen had been employed by Marshall. However, whilst Owen had been repairing the wheels of a farmer's cart, he had burnt them and so the owner refused to have them and sent them back. Marshall therefore did not pay Owen for this bodged work. Owen attacked Marshall and a fight broke out. Owen never received the money for the work which he thought was due to him, and later said to other people, 'There is a man near Uxbridge who owes me some money, and if I don't get it off him next time I go, I'll murder him.' He repeated this only two days before the murder. Presumably his spells in Reading Gaol and Cold Bath Fields prison prevented him from taking his revenge earlier than he did.

However, there is a rival theory which circulates in the family. This was that Owen was determined to marry Charlotte and so turned up on the day that the wedding dress was to have been delivered. When she refused him, he killed the entire family. This does not seem to tally with the known facts. A nocturnal visit seems an odd time for such a call – did Owen think she might elope with him? Witnesses certainly saw him in the early hours on his way back to Uxbridge.

A little more of his biography was learnt. He was the son of a tailor in Byfield, Northamptonshire. In more prosperous days, he married and had kept a beer house in Shipston-on-Stoor. However, he got into trouble with the law and lost his licence. In 1858 he deserted his wife and turned to a wandering life of villainy.

Owen had been the epitome of calm indifference throughout the trial. His callous attitude persisted until the end. Attempts by the prison chaplain, the Revd Mr Bumberry, towards him, were met with 'curses and foul expressions'. Later Owen claimed to be a Catholic, but when a priest from Wolverton was brought to him, he behaved just as he had with the Anglican minister, declaring he did not believe there was a God or devil, heaven or hell. At one point, he said, 'I am only sorry that I did not shoot Superintendent Dunham and a Justice of the Peace, that one sentenced me as well.' When his aged father and estranged wife visited him, he treated them coldly and responded to their tears thus, 'What have you to snivel for?'

Just before his execution, he asked to sleep in the coffin that had been made for him. Refusing to attend a last chapel service, he ate a last hearty dinner. After retiring on the night before the execution, at 9, he slept soundly and woke at 3. His breakfast saw him asserting his innocence and joking. The bell rang at 8 and Owen was tied up as he met the hangman in the corridor. Once on the scaffold, the steps of which he took two at a time, he made a short and final address, 'My friends, I am going to die for the murder of Charles – What's his name? I forget. Oh! Charles Marshall; but I am innocent.' He died almost instantly.

Owen must rank of one of the most callous and brutal murderers in British history. His victims probably outnumber those of the unknown Whitechapel killer of 1888. For contemporaries, Owen's crimes might have recalled the Ratcliff Highway murders, when a family were butchered in their London house in 1811. Yet Owen and his monstrous deed are almost unknown now. Perhaps that is as well. Such infamy has been blotted out. Yet his innocent victims deserve to be remembered. They were butchered without mercy and their number included three young children, a woman about to be wed and one aged woman. Francis William, the baby, grew to boyhood and lived in Uxbridge, but died of tuberculosis in 1886.

The only slight consolation was that the perpetrator paid with his life and met a richly merited fate. It has to be said, too, that Owen was incredibly stupid. Having committed the crime, he changed into clothes that were not his own and could be easily recognized by friends and relatives of the dead man. Furthermore, his pawning of some for his loot in Uxbridge, where he could be recognized, was another blunder. Finally, telling Coombes of his plan to go to Reading was another absurd error. Perhaps he was supremely confident in his ability to escape the law or perhaps he had a subconscious wish to be captured and punished? Or was he a monumental blockhead? Despite the praise the judge gave to Dunham, the detection involved in this case was minimal. It was fortunate for the police that Owen was so incredibly foolish, for lacking the aids of forensic science, tracking the killer would otherwise have presented a huge difficulty.

The Pall Mall Gazette, in 1870, made some comment about the liberals who were campaigning for the abolition of the death penalty, arguing that criminals could be reformed by enlightened work in prisons and would become useful members of society. The newspaper argued, however:

> does anyone believe that John Owen was capable of reformation? In the presence as such cases as this, all corrective theories disappear, and mankind is brought face to face with the supreme law of self preservation in which justifies us in abolishing John Owen as we would abolish a dangerous beast or reptile.

CHAPTER 12

The Hayes Tragedy, 1884

I am of opinion that the wound in the back of the shoulder could not have been inflicted by the man himself.

Mr James Gibbons, aged 63, was a contractor employed by the Great Western Railway Company for the creosoting of sleepers. Although he had worked as a labourer at Brentford Gas Works in 1851, he had done well for himself in later years. He had moved about too, being in Whitchurch, Devon, in 1861 and in West Ham in 1871. By 1884, he was fairly prosperous, employing a dozen men and owning several horses. He had resided in the village of Hayes, not far from the railway station, since 1877. Although married to Elizabeth who was nine years his junior, for thirty-seven years, they had no children. He was also a teetotaller and a prudent man, having paid his annual rent far in advance. He had £450 in savings. Although his wife had

Hayes Railway Station, 1914. Philip Sherwood's collection

worked in the past (in 1871 she was employed at a paper mill), from at least 1881 she does not seem to have been employed.

From early 1882 to October 1884, the two had lived with Lucy Venn, daughter of Mary Venn, a cousin of Gibbons, who was from Taunton (Gibbons was also a Devon man, being born in Culmstock). She was 15, and called the Gibbons uncle and aunt. She helped out around the house doing domestic chores. She recalled that the two were kind to her, but that Elizabeth liked a drink and could be quarrelsome afterwards. It was she who had decided that Lucy should return to her mother. Gibbons provided Lucy with money to attend school in order to fit her for a profession after she returned. On 14 November he wrote to the Venns to announce his intended visit to them on the following day. Therefore on Saturday 15 November 1884 he left home in the morning to visit relations in Taunton. He kissed his wife goodbye as he left their house.

Annie Hall, a girl who lived in Fleet Lane, Hayes, had been employed as a servant by the Gibbons for the past six weeks. Elizabeth ordered 6 pence worth of beer from the Royal Oak Beer house in Hayes. At 1 pm, she accompanied her mistress to Uxbridge. Whilst there Elizabeth had 4 pence worth of gin. Later in the afternoon and evening she had two and a half pints of ale.

Abraham Adams, the Hayes stationmaster, saw Gibbons return to the station at about 9.25 pm. Adams thought Gibbons seemed in good health and happy. He arrived home between 9.30 and 10, and had supper. By this time Annie had gone home (she did not sleep on the premises). Whilst undressing for bed at about 11, he and his wife had words. This was all the more dangerous because he kept a six-chambered revolver under his pillow.

Shortly afterwards Elizabeth ran screaming from the house, her clothes stained with blood. She called on her neighbour, Mrs Diana Sowman, and the two women returned to the Gibbons's house. Her husband was lying in the bedroom and appeared to be dead. Mr Parrott, a Hayes surgeon, was called for and, after arriving at midnight, he in turn called for the police. PC Hunt arrived and took possession of the revolver. Elizabeth seemed very distressed.

Hunt recalled that Elizabeth was in a state of 'great grief'. She then told him:

> Policeman, I can hardly realize it; it does not seem true. To see how he used to kneel by the chair and pray every night. He came home at about half past nine at night, and had supper and went out to look at the horse. He had then gone upstairs and partly undressed himself; I had gone up just before. I asked him whether Mary had met him, he having been to Taunton that day. His reply was 'Yes'. I said 'I think she might have written and told me'. He said, 'I do not know why she did not write'. And then he took the revolver from under the pillow, swung it round and fired it three or four times. He then fell to the floor, having been sitting on the bed.

Parrott and his assistant, Mr Hathaway found the deceased lying on the bedroom floor, between the door and the bed. He was obviously dead. This was due to the three bullet wounds on his person. One was in the middle of his left cheek. The others were on the left side of his body.

On the following day, Adams and William and George Weston, business colleagues of Gibbons, made a call on his house. Elizabeth told them about her husband's death.

Freeman's Lane, Hayes, the Gibbons's house is on the left. Philip Sherwood's collection

At the inquest, held at the Royal Oak, Elizabeth explained that her husband often excited himself, did not sleep well and was much depressed. Three or four years before he had had a bad fall and suffered from sunstroke. The implication was that he had shot himself. Dr Diplock, the coroner, was displeased that the body had been moved from its original position. He said it was important that the jurymen see the corpse in situ. Because there were no doctors present, he decided to adjourn the inquest until they could be present to give their evidence. The jury agreed.

On 24 November the inquest was resumed. Startling new evidence was given by Parrott which changed the nature of the whole enquiry. He told the court that he had subsequently made a post-mortem examination, with Hathaway's help. It was then that they found an additional wound. There was a bullet hole in the back of the left shoulder, midway between the spinal column and the point of the shoulder. It had passed in horizontally, to the depth of three inches, through soft tissues. He had not noticed the shoulder wound before, because he was inexperienced in dealing with gunshot wounds.

Diplock asked Parrott what his conclusion was. He replied,

Royal Oak, Hayes, c. 1900. Philip Sherwood's collection

I am of opinion that the wound in the back of the shoulder could not have been inflicted by the man himself. Five bullets were produced by the witness, who said that four were taken from the body, and the fifth given to him as one that had been picked up from the floor of the bedroom.

Mr Anthony Bowlby, surgical registrar at St Bartholomew's Hospital, concurred with his colleague's judgement that the shoulder wound could not have been self-inflicted. Any one of the wounds would probably have been sufficient for the deceased not to have fired another. Another witness was Alfred Pullman of Coldharbour Farm, Hayes, who was passing nearby on the fatal night. He had heard exclamations coming from the Gibbons's house and then someone rushing out, calling for Mrs Sowman, but did not see anyone.

Diplock concluded that, as Elizabeth was the only other person in the house on that night, the presumption must be, if the wounds were not self-inflicted, that she had been responsible for them. Inspector Daniel Morgan had her arrested and taken to Uxbridge Police Station, whilst his colleagues pursued their investigations. Meanwhile William Garner, an Uxbridge solicitor, looked to her interests.

On 1 December, at Uxbridge Town Hall before the magistrates, she was formally charged with murder. Parrott reiterated his evidence and said that he was prepared to swear on oath that Gibbons could not have shot himself through the shoulder. Morgan then presented the results of the police investigation. Initially he had believed it to be a case of suicide, but an examination of the deceased's shirt had convinced him otherwise. He said that, on questioning, Elizabeth had protested her innocence and maintained this after being arrested.

What had caused him to be suspicious was that he had found marks of blood behind the bedroom door. Parrott had hinted his suspicions to Morgan. He also thought Elizabeth's demeanour was suspect too when he had interviewed her in the presence of Mrs Sowman, Elizabeth's sister, and a constable. Morgan recalled: 'The prisoner answered my questions readily; I thought she was remarkably cool for a person placed in her position.'

Bowlby discussed his findings, and added that, unlike Parrott, he had had considerable experience in dealing with gunshot wounds, having dealt with between fifteen and twenty cases. He said this could not have been a case of suicide.

It was uncertain whether husband and wife were living on good terms. Ann Markham, who took the deceased's shirts away on the day after his death, said that the two always seemed to live happily together, but another school of thought was that the opposite was the truth. George Weston thought the two were only on 'middling' terms and, when pressed, admitted that they did not often agree.

The case was resumed at Uxbridge a week later. This time, Elizabeth's distress was all too clear; as she was 'sobbing convulsively throughout the hearing'. There was some additional evidence. Sergeant Mawby commented that an extra bullet had been found in the bedroom by Rose Harrison, Elizabeth's sister, but the last of the six bullets was too tightly jammed in the chamber and would not fire. Finally, the bench decided to commit Elizabeth for trial at the Old Bailey. She pleaded 'not guilty', but reserved her defence.

It was a two-day trial, beginning on 18 December. There was the suggestion that Gibbons's tragic death was indeed suicide. An aunt of his had killed herself following a disappointment in love. Another relation of his had to enter an asylum for the insane. Elizabeth recalled that her husband had complained of being unwell. However, Parrott stated that he had only seen Gibbons once in his professional capacity, when he was alive, and that was only due to a case of dyspepsia. He also thought that Gibbons was of a cheerful disposition.

Physical evidence was also considered. Gibbons was a right-handed man. He could not have inflicted the shoulder wound. The shots were fired at a very close range and there was blackening on his clothes where the bullets had entered. It also seemed a very strange method of committing suicide. Finally, there seemed no motive why he should do so.

However, there was a motive for Elizabeth to kill her husband. On 7 February 1881, Gibbons had made a new will, revoking all previous ones, and it left all his money and property to Elizabeth. The will was proved on 6 December

1884 and his personal estate was worth £435 16s 2d. Not a fortune, but certainly a sizeable sum.

The defence counsel spoke on the following day. He argued that there was no motive for murder. Elizabeth did not know the contents of her husband's will. He argued that the prosecution's case rested on the medical evidence alone. The jury did not need long to decide on guilt or innocence. They decided that Elizabeth was guilty within half an hour. The judge donned his black cap and pronounced the death sentence on her. She was then returned to Newgate. The execution was set for 5 January 1885.

William Garner, her solicitor, made strenuous efforts on her behalf. Two petitions were prepared to be presented to Sir William Harcourt, the Home Secretary. These were on the grounds that the conviction was unsafe. There was no motive for murder and suicide was more likely. They argued that the Gibbons were on good terms with one another. Over 200 people from Uxbridge, Hayes, Hillingdon, Cowley and West Drayton signed the petition in her favour. The prison chaplain visited Elizabeth and told her of the petitions, but warned her not to be too optimistic. Her nephew and niece from Hayes also visited her. The chairman of the jury who had sat in judgement wrote to the local paper, 'I was in court the whole of the trial and feel sure a fairer trial than could not be and the prisoner was most ably defended', though even he hoped that the sentence would be commuted to one of imprisonment.

Finally, on the last day of 1884, the prison governor was informed that the petitions had been received favourably and thus Elizabeth was reprieved and her sentence was transmuted to that of penal servitude for life, though life did not mean life (even before the 1960s). In 1891, she was a convict at a women's prison in Knaphill, Surrey. Yet in 1901 she was living with her niece at Cobden Road, Brighton. She did return to Hayes, but was shunned, despite many people having signed the petition in her favour in 1884. She died in about 1908.

It would seem though that this was a case of murder and that Elizabeth escaped the noose in part because of her sex. The question is why did she commit the crime? Was it for money? Her husband's will left all his property to her, but she was apparently unaware of this. She may have guessed, of course. Or was she tired of the marriage? There seems no indication that her husband was adulterous or violent, either. Another possibility, and perhaps the most likely, is that Elizabeth did not like her husband's interest in Lucy Venn. She had succeeded in having her removed from the household a few weeks before the murder, and when her husband tried to continue that relationship, she killed him. This is not to suggest that James was having an improper relationship with the young girl, though this cannot be entirely ruled out. But he was proposing to invest money in her education; money which perhaps Elizabeth did not think should be spent in such a way. This, together with her drinking during the fatal day, may have pushed her to the point where restraint gave way to violence.

CHAPTER 13

Who Murdered Sarah Higgs? 1895

Only think that while we have been wondering where she
was or where she could have got to, that she was lying
here in the canal within sight of our windows, only
50 yards away and we knew nothing about it.

For the middle classes the nineteenth century was a
golden age for servants. Most professional people, as
well as those of independent means, possessed at
least one; many had two or three domestic servants. These
were usually female, so could not command the wages of their
male equivalents. Kensington apart, in the late Victorian era,
Ealing had most servants per head of population. In 1911
there were 68 servants per 100 households, compared to 23
per 100 in London. The lot of servants was variable, but few
had such a fate as Sarah Jane Higgs.

The Lyric Theatre, Ealing Broadway, c. *1900.* Reg Eden's collection

In the Southall press, in late February 1895, came the following paragraph:

> At the beginning of last week much painful excitement was caused in Yiewsley and the surrounding locality, by the discovery, in the Grand Junction Canal, near Horton Bridge, of the dead body of Sarah Jane Higgs …

Sarah had been born in March 1871 at Yiewsley and her parents still resided there in 1895, at Thatcher's Cottages, near Horton Bridge, in a district then known as Starveall, which was notorious for its poverty. Her father was William, a labourer in a brickfield, and she had two older sisters. Since the summer of 1894, she had been employed as a housemaid at Mrs Josephine Draper's house at Mount Park Road, Ealing, and received an annual salary of £16, paid monthly. She appeared to be 'a quiet, well behaved, respectable young woman' and her mother said she was cheerful and industrious (it was and is very rare for anyone to say anything against the

Mount Park Road, Ealing, 2007. Author's collection

character of a murder victim). As a child she had attended the Church National School, leaving at 13. She had then worked as a servant in various posts – at Frank Potter's, the West Drayton stationmaster's, then in Uxbridge, then in London, before working in Ealing. Crucially, she had worked at a house in Hartington Road, Ealing, in 1891 (perhaps since 1889).

That her character was golden was not strictly true. She had given birth to an illegitimate son, one Henry John, on 4 October 1891, and the father (whose identity was not stated on the child's baptism record) acknowledged the baby as his, contributing towards its maintenance until the baby's death early in the following year. The father was unknown, but was said to be a man who lived near her mother's house, though this is not certain. Furthermore, she was three months pregnant at the time of death – or, as the newspapers delicately put it 'her mistress had reason to suspect her condition'. In fact, Mrs Draper had intended to speak to her on this matter.

She never got the chance. On the evening of Thursday 2 January 1895, after eating a hearty meal at 2 o'clock, Sarah left the house. At first this went unnoticed. Thursday was her usual evening off and she had talked to Matilda Baker, a fellow servant, of catching the 8.17 pm train to visit her parents at Yiewsley and to return by 10 o'clock, which was when she was required to be at her employer's. There would have been time for her to have made a short visit and then to return. West Drayton Station was and is only about ten minutes walk at most from where her parents lived. She had been wearing a round sailor hat, a dark dress and jacket and a white silk handkerchief. She also stated that the reason for the visit was to visit Emma Portman, a dressmaker there, but she said that she had not seen Sarah since August 1894.

What happened on the evening of 2 January is impossible to say with complete certainty. What is clear is that she did not travel by the 8.17 train, as she was seen in Ealing Broadway just before 9 o'clock. It would have then been impossible to have gone to Yiewsley and returned for 10. Such behaviour was unusual and Sarah had never done such before, except when she had to take a few days off in the previous August, due to illness. On the following day, Sarah's sister (who lived at Kilburn and had seen Sarah as recently as 30 December) came to Mrs Draper's house and took away Sarah's belongings, though no money was found, despite Sarah being said to be reasonably affluent. Mrs Draper found some medicine bottles in her employee's room and a half-finished letter to her half-sister, concerning some trinkets she planned to give to her. None of those who knew her at Yiewsley had seen her there. Meanwhile, the police made enquiries at lodging houses, without any positive result.

It was on 25 February that Thomas Clayton, butcher and fruiterer of Yiewsley High Street, made a shocking discovery. He had been walking along the canal towpath, near Horton Bridge, less than a hundred yards from where Sarah's mother lived, and saw what he at first thought to be bundle of rags floating in a gap in the ice-covered water. He thought nothing of it and passed by. However, on passing the same way again later in the day, he examined the object and found that it was a corpse. PC Cruickshank was summoned and took possession. Among the crowd who gathered there, a man shouted, 'There has been foul play here'. The corpse's outer skirt had been removed but otherwise it was fully clothed. The tragedy was noted by Martha Higgs, Sarah's mother, who said,

Horton Bridge, 2005. Author's collection

De Burgh Arms, 2005. Author's collection

'Only think that while we have been wondering where she was or where she could have got to, that she was lying here in the canal within sight of our windows, only 50 yards away and we knew nothing about it.'

No money had been found on the body, though there was a small silver brooch. Apparently, shortly before her disappearance, Sarah had received a postal order for an unknown amount and from an unknown source.

The inquest was held later that day at the De Burgh Hotel, which was and is very near to West Drayton railway station. After having identified the body and having heard from Martha that the family had not seen her since August 1894 when Sarah had been ill, the main point under discussion was the cause of death. Dr William Hayden of Wycombe House, Yiewsley, said that the face and the lower part of the body were covered in mud from the bottom of the canal, but he thought that the corpse had not been held down in it. It was only slightly decomposed. He had also found, on closer examination, that there was a frontal head wound about $1\frac{1}{2}$ inches long, which had broken one bone and fractured another. There was also a wound at the back of the head, which had not broken any bones. These blows had been inflicted when Sarah was alive, by a fall or a blow. She had not drowned, as there was no water in the lungs, but had been in the water for at least six weeks. The stomach was healthy, but there was no food in it. She was three months pregnant. The inquest was then adjourned in order to ascertain Sarah's last movements and to gather other pertinent information.

The adjourned inquest, which took place at the same location, but at which the police were present, was held a week later. Detective Inspector Nash and his colleagues had been making investigations. The adjourned inquest lasted three hours. A number of witnesses were questioned.

The first was Mary Farr, a servant at Eccleston Road, Ealing Dean. She reported that she was a friend of Sarah's and that they often spent their leisure time together. On 16 December, on their way back from Acton, they met a man whom Sarah referred to as her 'young man', but Mary did not know his name. On the night of her disappearance they had met in Ealing Broadway at 8.20 and walked to Ealing Common railway station, then back, meeting another female friend outside the Lyric Theatre on Ealing Broadway. Mary left them at about 9.15. She could not identify the man seen on 16 December, as she had only seen the back of his head. He was about 30, had been wearing a light coat, black felt hat and black trousers; possibly he worked in a shop. She added that Sarah seemed cheerful and did not think anything out of the usual was in the offing.

One Martha Batt, a friend of Sarah's, recalled, 'She said she was going to West Drayton with someone. She did not mention any name, but I expected it was her young man.' Apparently Sarah had had a knowing look.

William Hammond, labourer of St. Mary's Cottages, Yiewsley, stated that he had seen Sarah loitering near Horton Bridge early one morning, apparently looking for a lost possession – perhaps her outer skirt. He had known her for five years, but claimed he had never spoken to her, as 'I have got enough to do with the one at home'. When he returned to the same spot, twenty minutes later, she had vanished. Unfortunately he did not remember on what day it was, only 'after Christmas'.

Charles Butler of 3 Eastwood's Cottages, Yiewsley, who was possibly a labourer, had walked out with Sarah on three occasions in the summer of 1894. The last was on the August Bank Holiday. He had been with her and Ada, his sister, to the Lyric Theatre but, though 'we were friendly towards each other', he stressed that 'he was never guilty of any improper conduct' with her and that he 'did not know much' about her. He had not seen her since and did not know if she was seeing another man.

It certainly seems that Sarah was seeing another man and was on intimate terms with him. Ellen Downes, a servant working at 22 Eaton Rise, and an old friend of Sarah's, said that Sarah intended to visit the Metropolitan Music Hall on Boxing Day 1894 and she was not going alone. She had expected to see Sarah on 30 December, but had not. Sarah's sister said that she knew who she was walking out with and referred to him as 'the biggest scamp out'. She did not identify him. This other man had been friends with Sarah since at least November, and this man was not Charlie. Charlie was clearly Charles Butler, as a servant recalled that Sarah said she had not seen him since August, which agrees with Charles's own account. There was uncertainty whether the man in question was from Ealing or not. Ellen certainly thought so, but others disagreed.

One possible clue – or red herring – came from Algernon Goodenough, booking clerk at West Drayton Station. He said that at 11 pm on 19 January, he had heard a woman's screams from the direction of Horton Bridge. He thought it might be a domestic assault, though another witness said they were merely noises made by rowdy youths leaving a nearby pub, probably the Trout or the Chequers. When Goodenough saw two constables, they said that the route was not on their beat, so could not investigate. Yet it was believed that Sarah had been starved for two weeks before entering the water, which would tally with Goodenough's statement.

Dr Hayden, who had had time to make another examination, was able to give further evidence. Another fracture at the front of the head wound was found. He said that the cause of death was shock to the nervous system from concussion to the brain and spinal cord, being caused by the blow to the back of the head. The body had been in the water for some time and so it was impossible to tell if all the blows had been made at the same time. There was some debate as to whether the death was suicide, caused by Sarah leaping from the bridge and hitting her head on the side of the bridge. Hayden said that Sarah was unconscious, but not dead when she entered the water. The jury only needed a short consultation before reaching the verdict of 'Wilful murder against some person or persons unknown'. Her mother was 'sure Sarah had been murdered and that she had been lured down there for that purpose'.

The killer was never found. The motive for the murder, though, is clear enough. Sarah was pregnant and she had told the prospective father about it. He was not in a position to marry her, or did not wish to do so. Perhaps he was already married or was in a situation in which the scandal of the result of his illicit affair would have been harmful. Could Sarah have been trying to blackmail him? He may have met her at the Lyric on 2 January, and suggested she go to West Drayton with him. Or perhaps he suggested elopement or marriage? This would tie in with the absence of money in her room, as he may

St Matthew's Church, Yiewsley, 2007. Author's collection

have suggested she take it with her. Having lured her there, he must have held her prisoner somewhere (but where? – perhaps a shed or outhouse – certainly nowhere that anyone might conceivably visit) for about two weeks, before deciding on what he should do. It is possible that 19 January was the date of the murder and, having wounded her, he threw her from the bridge, where she sank. The delay in the body being discovered was caused by the frosty weather, with ice covering the canal until late February.

Who killed her? Probably not Charles Butler, who had not seen her for months, though he did live near to the scene of the crime. William Hammond? Possibly, but probably not. He had motive (being married already) and was near the scene of the crime. He was vague about when he saw her, though this is not necessarily a sign of guilt, but merely bad memory. He may have been her lover, but the question remains about where he hid her and how she could have been hidden for so long. As both men were labourers, they would not have resembled the shopkeeper's assistant who had been identified as Sarah's beau – unless, of course, they had changed into their Sunday best as one would when courting. It is a pity that Sarah's sister did not name her current lover.

Or could the killer have been Frank Potter, the stationmaster whom she had worked for in the mid-1880s? He had been born in 1856 and by 1891 was a married man with five children, and lived in West Drayton throughout this period (1881–1901). Some thought that her killer lived locally. He certainly knew Sarah and would have been in the right place at the right time; nor would he in a position to marry the pregnant Sarah. All this, is, of course, very circumstantial and does not provide any real evidence.

Yet there was one more suspect, and a far more promising one. Although his identity was unknown, he was described thus:

Height 5 ft. 8 in., black hair, dark moustache, with little side whiskers. He wore a brown golf cap, and carried a slate covered waterproof coat on his left arm, was attired in a brownish tweed frock coat, dark striped, trousers and gaiters.

His name was Harold and he was married, with five children, and bore 'a good position'. He had been 'keeping company' with Sarah for two years, having seduced her and spoke to her of marriage. Sarah's baby was Henry, so it is not unlikely that the father could have been named Harold. Apparently he was seen with her on the morning of her disappearance at a pub in Little Ealing, presumably the Plough, by a page boy who worked in Mount Park Road. He may have been the same man that Mary Farr saw in the previous month. Yet is this story true? Why was Sarah in Little Ealing, nearly two miles from where she worked? It seems a long way (at least half an hour's walk) to go on an errand or with a message for her mistress.

Who was Harold? An examination of the young men named Harold who were householders in Ealing in 1891 only comes up with two names. One was Harold Lavey, but he was unmarried in 1891, and the second was Harold Pryke and, although married, had no children. Both seem to be ruled out, therefore. However, there is another and more probable man. This is Harry Dicconson, born in Canada and aged 39 in 1891, a commercial traveller, married and with seven children. Crucially, he was Sarah's employer at Hartington Road in 1891. He had resided in Ealing, and at this address, since about 1889. He certainly meets all the criteria listed by witnesses. Furthermore, as Sarah's employer, he would be able to exert a strong influence over her and sexual relations between masters and servants were not unknown. The Plough is about a mile from his home, so might have been a convenient meeting place for them. The only argument against him being her killer is that he seems a little old to be described as a young man, when he would have been 42 in 1895. Dicconson left Ealing in about 1899 and by 1901 resided in Barnes, Surrey.

The other question concerns motivation. Did Sarah expect her lover to settle down with her? Or did she intend the dangerous game of blackmail? Did the man plan to kill her, anyway, or was his hand forced by threats of exposure?

We do not know whether the police questioned Dicconson. No more was learnt in public of any police investigation which surely must have followed the announcement at the inquest, and the police file on the case does not exist. Nevertheless, Dicconson seems the most likely suspect.

Chapter 14

Murder or Suicide? 1899

I told him I was an inspector of police and that I should take him into custody on suspicion of having murdered his wife by throwing her into the Grand Junction Canal.

It was an apparently pleasant evening in May of 1899. William Perryman, a 22-year-old labourer of the High Street, Uxbridge, remembered it well, and recalled thus:

On the 23rd inst., I came out of my house. I was going for a walk to give my dog a run. I went out of doors a little before 10 o'clock at night. I had not got five or six yards when I heard a violent scream … I took no more notice of the scream: I thought it was perhaps someone over the bridge having a bit of a row. I took no more notice after that. I walked along and filled my pipe and walked quietly on the bridge. Being a nice night I looked over and saw something move in the water … Then the scream came back to my mind. I thought there must be someone in the water. I turned round and saw two men coming up the hill from the 'Swan and Bottle' side. I said 'I believe there is someone in the water'.

Perryman knew one of the men. He continued his account:

We rushed round to Mr Steven's side of the wharf … One of them tried to have a look. He said, 'I don't believe there is anything there'. I said, 'Well, I am certain I saw something'. He said, 'What shall we do? I can't swim'. I rushed round to get to the tow-path side, and I said, 'I am going in to see'. I went over as quickly as possible on to the tow-path and took off some clothes, and went in at the spot where I thought was most likely. Of course it had shifted. I made a grab at something I thought was something like, and it turned out a bunch of weeds or something of that sort. I shouted to the other two and said, 'It is nothing now', but to make sure I swam round and went under twice. I think the third time I got hold of something.

The discovery was shocking indeed, as Perryman concluded:

Well, I went under, being in the water I went under. I caught hold of the body and took it to the tow path ... I am not sure who it was who pulled the body out. That is all I saw. I was there some time because I had to dress as soon as I got out. There were plenty there to do what was wanted.

The body was that of a young woman, who was soon identified as being Mrs Rosetta Tilbury, aged 18 and married to one Charles George Tilbury, a 20-year-old labourer who was also a corporal in the Oxfordshire Militia.

Dr John Ferris of Uxbridge was soon summoned. He arrived at about 9.50 and later recalled:

I was called to see the body of a woman just taken out of the water. She was apparently dead. For half an hour I tried artificial respiration without effect – she never breathed once. Afterwards her body was removed to a shed and I thoroughly examined the body that night and on the inside of her right hand, which had a pocket handkerchief tied round it, found a most distinct cut ... done by a knife; a very small wound. I could find no other bruising that night but on Thursday I found a slight bruise in front of each elbow and a small mark behind the left ear, but I thought it was post mortem. One witness said she thought she saw a bruise behind her left ear. I thought it was post mortem. I have since made a post mortem. I am of the opinion she died of drowning. The liver was rather hard, but had nothing to do with the cause of death.

PC White recalled:

I remember the Tuesday evening in question. I was called to the canal side at about 10.15. I there saw Dr Ferris examining a dead woman. She had a long black ulster on; shortly after the body was removed to the stables of The Swan and Bottle. Here the woman was stripped. I took charge of the clothing, which I now produce; a black ulster bodice, skirt, hat and underclothing, and the only thing found in her pocket was the knife produced.

Her husband was arrested on suspicion of having murdered her by drowning. In order to try and understand this tragedy, we need to look at the events leading up to it.

Charles Tilbury had been born in High Wycombe, Buckinghamshire, in about 1879; his father Henry was variously recorded as being a gamekeeper and a publican. In 1891 Tilbury was a farm labourer living in Great Marlowe. Five years later he was living at Wycombe and was employed by Horace Roberts, contractor and carter. It was there and at this time that he met Rosetta, who was two years his junior and described as 'a very good-looking young lady, of a lively disposition'. She was from Wycombe, too. He recalled, 'I knew her some time before I married her. At the time I married my wife I knew her not to bear a morally good character.' They were married at Brentford Registry Office in October 1897 when Rosetta claimed her age was 20.

They lived together in a house at Hanwell. Tilbury's purpose was to remove her 'from those with whom she had been associated, and to give her a fresh start'. They lived there happily enough until the summer of 1898. Tilbury left his wife for a month to attend his annual militia training. On his return from the camp, he was told by Rosetta's sister that his wife had been seeing a Greenford man. She admitted her unfaithfulness, but he forgave her. However, she later 'stayed out all night with him again, across the Greenford fields'. Sometimes Rosetta would get drunk with her neighbours, and her husband would threaten to strike her, but never actually hit her. Often he had to make his own tea. The couple moved westwards and began to live at Colham Green, Hillingdon. This was a strange neighbourhood to her, but not to him, and again, Tilbury hoped he had removed his wife from temptation.

At the beginning of 1899, they were living with a Mrs Tyrell at Colham Green, but by March they had moved to Eunice Tilbury's, who was a very distant relation, though some said she was his aunt. In March and early April, matters seemed to go better as Rosetta avoided drink. Yet on the evening of 16 April, her husband was returning from work and was told by Mrs Tyrell that his wife was with others in the Windsor Castle pub. Two days later, after having worked for a drainage contractor, Tilbury came home at six and could not find his wife. No one seemed to know where she was. He said to Mrs Tilbury, 'This is not the first time she has been away like this.' He went with a friend to Uxbridge to look for her there, after saying to Mrs Tilbury, 'She will have something when she gets home'. He was warned not to knock her about and he agreed. His wife did not return that night and someone said she had gone to Langley and Slough.

On the following day Tilbury did not go to work, but went to West Drayton, presumably to catch the train westwards. He looked for his wife in Slough and Maidenhead, but without success, so returned to West Drayton. At the Forrester's Arms he learnt that his wife had visited there earlier that day. When he arrived home, it was 7 and he saw his wife there. She said that she would not do it again. Tilbury was firm with her, but later denied he used any physical violence.

In the following month it was again time for Tilbury's militia training. He left home on 13 May and arrived at camp at Buckingham on the following day. Corporal Briden was in the same company as Tilbury. They talked, but Briden did not know anything about Tilbury's wife, or even that he was married. However, on 20 May, Tilbury received the following letter from his wife, written two days earlier and posted on the previous day:

My dear and loving husband,
I am now writing a few lines in answer to your kind letter as I was very pleased to hear from you and we are pleased you reached there quite safe dear Ben try and catch a train

as early as you can there is not time for you to write another
letter or you could have told me what time and then we
could have come meet you dear ben I am still at work and
getting on all right and I hope you are the same and make
your self look as nice as you can try and borrow a sash I have
got such a cold I can hardly speak we shall be at home both
of us when you come dear Ben we will have more
conversation when you come home your Aunt is pretty
queer just now I am going to bed and get up in the morning
this is Thursday night I received your letter on Wednesday
night I think this is all at present for a short time Good night
God protect you now you are away from your loving wife.

R. Tilbury

Pield Heath Hillingdon near Uxbridge, Middlesex

Xxxxxxxxxxx

Tilbury decided that he would have to travel to see his wife
straight away. Briden was on guard duty that Saturday
afternoon, and recalled that Tilbury said to him, 'Briden, will
you do my picket tonight? If you'll do my picket tonight, I'll
give you a shilling for doing it for me.' Briden replied, 'Well,
it's like this here, if you can get leave from the sergeant major,
I'll do it for you.' Tilbury said, 'I want to go and see my missus'
and 'If I don't get a pass, I'll take French leave'.

Tilbury went without permission, arriving back at his
lodgings in Hillingdon on the following evening, Saturday 20
May. Hearing she was in Uxbridge, he found her at the Eight
Bells at 10.40. She had been drinking with one William
Adeway, who asked, 'Is this the young man you were talking of
to my wife?' Rosetta said, 'This is my husband'. At which,
Tilbury threatened to hit her. They went to the Windsor Castle
pub on Kingston Lane, but it was closed, so the married
couple went home and Tilbury locked her inside. She wanted
to leave to see the men outside, but her husband put her to
bed.

On the following day she asked him for a bottle. Finding it
contained poison, Tilbury asked, 'What are you going to do
with it?' She replied, 'I am tired of my life. I shall take some
when you are gone out to be out of the way.' On the Monday

St Lawrence's Church, Cowley, 2005. Author's collection

evening the two went to the Windsor Castle. Rosetta was asked
to sing by one of the other patrons. Tilbury was annoyed and
said: 'She won't sing, she belongs to me.' He offered to fight
anyone who encouraged her to disobey him. They then went
home, but were followed and one man hit Tilbury. The latter
fled and hid in Mrs Tilbury's woodhouse and was not found
by his pursuers. Rosetta was with Daniel Russell (who later
admitted knowing Rosetta in Greenford – perhaps he had
been her lover then?) and Adeway. It seems they slept rough
near the brickfields by Cowley church.

The three spent much of the following day together. Whilst
drinking at the Windsor Castle, a glass broke and Rosetta
injured her hand. Adeway left them at about five in the
afternoon. Rosetta collected a parcel from Mrs Cook, a dressmaker, and went with Russell to Uxbridge. Rosetta wanted to
pawn the costume in the parcel, but arrived too late at the
shop.

Tilbury asked his landlady on the following morning
(Tuesday 23 May) what had become of his wife. 'I have not
seen her since last night', she helpfully replied. Tilbury went to
Uxbridge railway station and applied for a pass to travel to
Buckingham, presumably to return to the militia camp. This

was refused (Tilbury needed a pass as he had no money). He also visited the police station, and Sergeant Green told him that he could not help. Finally he went towards Harlington Fair to look for his wife. He then walked around West Drayton and Pield Heath. He could not find his wife and asked Mrs Tilbury where she was. He returned to Uxbridge. It was now about 6. At the Market Place he asked a man where his wife was and set off towards Hillingdon.

Rosetta was with Daniel Russell, who left her on Tilbury's arrival. She was carrying a parcel with a dress in it. When Rosetta collected it, she told Mrs Cook that she was moving from the district because 'I am sure my husband means doing for me'.

It was now about 8. Tilbury told her he was going to Beaconsfield and she refused to go there or to Wycombe. The two argued. He took the parcel from her. Then she agreed to go halfway to Wycombe with him. They arrived at Uxbridge and they visited the police station. It was about 9. Rosetta said that she wished to apply for a separation order to escape her husband. When Green asked why, she said, 'My husband has been beating me about.' There were no marks of violence, so the unimpressed policeman told her to see the magistrate.

Uxbridge High Street, 1900s. Author's collection

Tilbury told him that his wife was always going out and would not lead a domestic life. Green then told Tilbury to return to camp. Green thought both had been drinking.

They walked by Market Place and then to the Eagle, arguing constantly. According to Tilbury, she said: 'I shall drown myself or do away with myself some way.' He replied: 'You have no reason to say that or do it.' They then walked over the swing bridge towards New Denham, passing a number of people, none of whom Tilbury could recall. They then parted, but soon rejoined one another and walked near to the Dog and Duck, but did not go in as he was penniless, and walked towards Ivy House Farm.

It was at about 9.30 that the two parted. Tilbury recalled:

> We parted on good terms. We shook hands, kissed, and she promised to let me know when she got a job. I walked as far as the Denham Avenue, got over the hedge and sat down against a tree. I went to sleep and woke up through the passing of a van. I knew the driver and asked for a lift to Beaconsfield.

William Keen, a High Wycombe man, was the driver. He recalled that Tilbury said to him: 'I have been to Uxbridge to see my friends'. Keen replied that he would need to return to army camp as he would be in trouble.

Tilbury went to a pub in Buckingham on 24 May. By chance, Briden met him there. He told him, 'Tilbury, you are doing something this time, aren't you? You'll "cop it" when you get to camp.' Tilbury replied, 'I don't trouble. I can do the bit.' In the mean time, Tilbury wrote a letter:

> My dear Aunt [Mrs Tilbury], I now right a few lines to you hoping to find you quite well as it is leaves me allright at present and I do hope and pray that rose came home quite safe that on Tuesday night allright and I saw my wife in Uxbridge and she went with me as far as the dog and duck along the bottom and right and tell me if she is at your place allright and I have not had my case over yet and think this is all this time from your ever loving George Tilbury so good

buy God bless you for ever and give my love to my Dear
Rose if she is here so good buy'.

Xxxxxxxxxxxx

Tilbury later went to the barracks at High Wycombe and
Sergeant Sherlock recalled seeing him there at 10 am on 24
May. Tilbury said to him, 'I am absent from the regiment since
the 20th inst.' Sherlock replied, 'Alright sir, I'll keep you here.'
Tilbury was then to be sent to the camp by the 3.18 train.
Tilbury also said, 'I shall be lucky if I get away because I
expect a policeman after me.'

Briden was put in charge of Tilbury until Thursday
afternoon. He told Tilbury that there was news that there had
been a drowning near Uxbridge. He said: 'You ain't drowned
your old woman?' Tilbury replied, 'I knows nothing about it.'
Briden thought Tilbury was astonished by the news, but not
was grief-stricken. He seemed not to believe it and treated it
as a joke.

For Tilbury, however, it was no jest. Later that afternoon,
Detective Inspector Cullagh Scott appeared at the camp. He
told him that he was a police inspector and had come to take
him into custody on suspicion of having killed his wife. Tilbury
remained as calm as ever. He was taken to Harrow Road
police station and then to Uxbridge on the following day.

The wheels of justice begin to move rapidly thereafter. On
Friday 26 May the magistrates began to examine the matter at
Uxbridge Town Hall. It was brief. Two witnesses, one being
Perryman, gave their evidence. Scott recounted his arrest of
Tilbury. The magistrates remanded Tilbury in custody until
the inquest on the following day.

A number of witnesses gave their accounts of the fatal night
at the inquest on 27 May. Francis Brooks, railway clerk, who
lived in George Street, Uxbridge, recalled:

I had been out in the direction of Denham, cycling. I was at
the canal bridge at ten minutes past nine. I got off my
bicycle and walked towards Messrs Osborne and Stevens'
timber yard. When opposite the yard I saw a soldier in
uniform and a woman. He was a short soldier. They

appeared to me to be having a drunken squabble. The woman appeared to be very excited and was using very bad language. I did not stop to hear their conversation, but went on.

Charles Langton, another Uxbridge man, recalled seeing the two at about 9.20, and that they were arguing. He recognized Tilbury as the man. Mrs Julia King of New Denham recalled having seen the two, also between 9.40 and 9.45. They were quarrelling.

Another important witness was Barbara Emmett, who lived in Harefield. She saw the couple at the bridge and recalled:

I have seen the young girl before. She had a brown paper parcel. Her husband was trying to take it away from her. They had hold of one another's necks and she screamed. I could not see whether he was biting her or hitting her ... He asked her if she was coming with him. They seemed as if they were going up the lane, but they turned back again. That is all I saw then. I saw them again when I was going home towards Harefield between a quarter and ten minutes to ten as near as I can guess. I saw them go across the canal bridge on to the towing path.

She went on to remark that she did not hear any screams or cries, but then she was a little deaf.

Alfred Spencer, one of the men whom Perryman had seen on the night of the tragedy, was called as a witness. He and a friend had been at the Swan and Bottle from 9 onwards. At about 9.35, they left and he recalled:

then I came out and my friend with me. He went round to the back and I waited for him just close to the bridge. I heard a scream. I did not take any part because I thought it was perhaps someone having a game under the bridge.

His friend also heard the noise and the two investigated. He then confirmed much of Perryman's story.

The Swan and Bottle Pub, Uxbridge, c. 1900. Author's collection

Mrs Tilbury told the court about the couple lodging with her. She was convinced that Tilbury ill-treated his wife, but never did it in her presence. Apparently he had once hit her and she had seen the bruise on her face, and he had once threatened her with a knife. He apparently said, 'if I do find her, I have something in my pocket and I'll run it through her'. He also was seen sharpening a knife, allegedly so he could cut some meat. However, he was noted as being a sober man.

Tilbury was then invited to speak, but on advice declined to do so. The jury went away to consider their verdict and returned in five minutes. Mr Hall, the foreman announced, 'We find that Rosetta Tilbury was found drowned, but there is not sufficient evidence to show how she came into the water.'

On 29 May, Rosetta was buried in Uxbridge Cemetery. There were no mourners present because her relatives were unaware of where the ceremony was taking place and when. Oddly enough, Perryman was one of the pall bearers.

The mystery gave rise to a great deal of comment. One press report noted: 'Rumours have been freely floated concerning the sad occurrence, and great speculation has prevailed among many of the inhabitants since the issue of the "Dailies" containing some startling particulars.' There was even a tale that there had been a large pool of blood on the towpath where the body had been found. However, this was nothing but the red dye from Rosetta's dress.

It was on 4 June that the magistrates continued their examination of the case. Mr Bird, an Uxbridge solicitor, represented the accused man. The jury were shown photographs and maps of the scene of the alleged crime to help them in their inquiry. At the end of the hearing, the magistrates concluded that no jury would convict under the circumstances and therefore dismissed the prisoner. Tilbury was loudly cheered by a large crowd who had gathered outside, but none were happier than his parents, and he was soon wearing a new suit of clothes. Two years later he was recorded as living in High Wycombe as a wheelwright.

Was Tilbury rightfully cleared? If he did not kill his wife by throwing her into the canal, what happened? She may have committed suicide, as she had allegedly threatened to do, though we only have her husband's word for that. Or he may have killed her. He certainly had motive enough, having quarrelled with her over her seeing other men, going missing and getting drunk. They had been quarrelling shortly before her death. And he did mention to Briden about the police being after him before any reference was made about the death of his wife. The great point is that no one had seen how Rosetta entered the water. Such slender circumstantial evidence would be insufficient grounds to send Tilbury to the Old Bailey for trial.

CHAPTER 15

Dreadful Murder at Yiewsley, 1899

*If ever Sherlock Holmes existed in real life, here is a case
where he would have an ample field.*

Yiewsley, as we have already seen, witnessed one murder in the 1890s. It was to see another, four years later. This was only a small village, with a population of 3,213 in 1901 and having two murders in the same decade must have seemed a rather large number. As with the death of Sarah Higgs, no one was ever found to have been responsible.

On the Saturday morning of 18 November 1899, young Belch, an apprentice, was on his way to work at Mr Smith's. It was about 5.50. He was walking along Providence Road, not far from the High Street, and where the new Baptist church was being built. It was there that he saw a man's feet and legs. Thinking the man was drunk, he mentioned this to the works' foreman, who made further enquiries. PC Bullin was the first on the scene, but did not touch anything and called for the doctor. On examination by Dr Hayden, it was obvious that the man was not drunk, but dead, and his face had been battered and mutilated. These injuries were not self-inflicted. PC Pengelly removed the corpse to the De Burgh Arms. He then searched it and found two 2 shilling pieces, a scrap of paper with £1 5s written on it, a pipe and a tobacco box.

The inquest was convened on Tuesday 21 November at the De Burgh Arms. This had been where the inquest on Sarah Higgs had been held almost five years before. Some of the same people were present on both occasions. Reginald Kemp, deputy county coroner was there, for one, as was Thomas Clayton, a local shopkeeper, who had first seen Miss Higgs's corpse and was now sitting on the jury; and finally, Dr Hayden, who was to pronounce on the cause of death in both cases.

Edgar Road, 2007. Author's collection

Alfred Theodore Cliff of Hambrook Villas, Edgar Road, Yiewsley was the first witness to be called. He identified the corpse. It was of his elder brother, William Thomas Cliff, who had only come to Yiewsley in June 1899, having travelled south from Salford. William Cliff had been born in Aldershot, the son of a soldier, but by 1891 was employed as a clerk at a dyeing works in Salford. His subsequent whereabouts is unknown – he does not seem to have been in England in 1881 (perhaps he had joined the army and was serving abroad). He had taken lodgings in the same street as his 38-year-old brother and his occupation was that of a mixer, employed at Para Rubber Works.

Dr Hayden was next. He had never seen the deceased until he had been called to examine the corpse just before 7 the previous Saturday morning. Hayden pointed out that the dead man had been lying on his back and that the body was cold. Life had been extinct for at least six or seven hours, possibly longer. When asked about the nature of the horrific injuries, he replied, 'All the bones of the face, except the nasal bone and the upper jaw bone and the lower jaw bone' were broken. They could not have been the result of a fall, unless that fall had been over twenty feet.

Providence Road, 2007. Author's collection

Yet the murder weapons were easy to identify, and the answer was soon coaxed out of the doctor by the coroner. There had been four or five bricks covered in blood about two or three feet from the corpse. Blood from the corpse could not have flowed to the bricks, because blood had not flowed above a foot from the body. The bricks were also very hard. Hayden then testified that he had left the scene once the police had arrived to take over.

Mr Roberts, the police surgeon, then gave his evidence. He agreed with all that his medical colleague had said. Then he proceeded to tell the court that he had made a post-mortem examination of the body. It had been in good health and there was no alcohol in the corpse. He then mentioned other injuries. A tooth was missing and was found nearby, and there was a small mark on his left wrist. His clothing was in disarray and was bloodstained. There was also a small wound to the back of the head. This was probably caused by a fall. Death was due to 'shock to the system, resulting from the fearful injuries and loss of blood'.

Alfred Cliff was then recalled to give further evidence. He explained about his late brother's personality and habits. His drinking habits came under scrutiny. Alfred said that he had been 'Very quiet. He liked his glass, but when he had drink he was not obstreperous ... When he could have it, he would have it and a very little knocked him over.' Although the victim got easily drunk (on only two pints), he did not become violent thereafter.

William was not walking out with any young woman, according to Alfred. He did not know that his brother had any enemies nor that he had quarrelled with anyone. Yet he had been asked to leave his lodgings on account of his drinking.

William had been given his weekly wage of 25 shillings at 6.30 that Friday evening, 17 November. He was then seen by his brother, alone, in the lobby of the Anchor, on Horton Road, at about 10. He was sober and bought ginger beer for Alfred and his friend, Mr Pratt. William then left, returning at about 10.30.

Alfred then said that he and Pratt had last seen his brother at about 11, not long before his death. They had all been just outside the Anchor. William had been drinking, but could walk without difficulty. He said he was about to return to Mother Gray's, where he was lodging. It was now 'turning out' time and men were leaving the said pub. One of them began to talk to William.

It had not been a dark night and the moon gave some light; enough for Alfred to take a look at the man who spoke to his brother. This man wore an overcoat and was tall. He wore a flat-top soft felt hat. When asked what the man's occupation might have been, or whether he was a labourer or not, he could give no reply. He would not recognize him if he saw him again. William then walked in the direction of the canal, via the High Street. And that was the last time Alfred saw his brother alive.

Joseph Coxwell, timekeeper at the works where William was employed, spoke next. He described the deceased as 'a very quiet and inoffensive man'. He recalled paying William his wages on the Friday, but had no idea about how he spent his money. He said that the paper on the body was merely the receipt he gave every man once he paid him. Alfred added that his brother did not save much money, having only 2 shillings in the savings bank.

Mrs Hankey, landlady of the Trout, recalled her deceased customer, agreeing that he was 'a very quiet man. I have never seen him the worse for liquor.' Apparently William had arrived at the Trout just after he had been paid at 6.30. William had

The pub that was formerly the Anchor, Yiewsley High Street, 2007. Author's collection

two pints. Although there were other men in the pub, he did not talk to anyone. Yet he left with some of them, with whom he seemed on friendly terms. Mrs Hankey did not know if William was particularly well off.

William's landlady since 28 August was Mrs Edith Mary Wilkinson. Whilst agreeing that her late lodger was a quiet man, she said that he often returned home the worse for wear, after having been drinking. She had become so exasperated that on 13 November she had given him notice to quit. She had last seen him at 8.15 on the Friday, when he had arrived at her house, a little drunk. He then had his not very substantial tea, consisting of bloater and bread and butter. According to her, he was in the habit of spending most of his money. There had been some words between them. William had asked her if she disliked him and she said no. He then said:

– What do you want me to go for, mother?
– Because you get drunk and leave the doors open so often.
– Very well: I'll look round and you'll leave the door open for me won't you?

She agreed and he left at 9. She later saw him near the Anchor, whilst she was out visiting a friend.

More evidence was given about his drinking habits. Mabel Brown, who lived in the Anchor, added that William was a regular there, and often came in before work, as well. She recalled his visit on the last Friday. She agreed that he was a quiet man, as did George Betteridge, landlord of the Red Cow. He said that William was never quarrelsome and recalled seeing him in that fatal Friday at his pub. It was suggested by a Mr Walding that William had gone to this pub after 11, but Betteridge had no knowledge of this. He said that he would not have been served after hours. Other witnesses attested to having seen William staggering home after 11.

Charles Martin, who had retired early on the Friday, and lived near to where the corpse had been found, recalled that he had heard a noise at about 2.25 on the following morning. He thought it was 'as of tumbling stones in Providence Road. I did not pay any particular attention to it as it is not an unusual thing, there being one or two dogs about.'

Mr Walding was recalled and he repeated that he and William had had a drink in the Red Cow after 11. Walding was the man who had met William outside the Anchor at about 11. He said that William left and walked towards the canal bridge. Walding then walked with Mr Fitzpatrick towards the Yiewsley Working Men's Club. He recalled having met a policeman on that night, too, before returning home just after midnight.

Finally, there was evidence given about William's work situation. Several men had been dismissed from the works that summer, and in June, William, through his brother's

Yiewsley High Street, c. *1900s.* Author's collection

recommendation, had been employed in the stead of one Mr Clifford, who, it appeared, had been sacked by mistake. Mr Nicholls, representing the works, did not think there had been any bad feeling against William because of this, however. Thomas Clayton agreed, stating: 'I would say there had been no disagreeableness between employer and employed there.'

All the evidence had been heard. Kemp then made his summing up:

> Well Mr Foreman and gentlemen, that is the whole of the evidence. It has been gone very carefully into and all we have heard seems to have made the matter more a mystery than ever. Deceased seems to have been a quiet and inoffensive man and even in drink he was not quarrelsome. We cannot discover that he had any particular enemy or anybody who had a grudge against him. There is no evidence that there is a woman in the case or that anybody had any jealousy against him. There is no sign that it was robbery; he had not much on him and all the money he is supposed to have had is fairly accounted for.

The jury returned a verdict of murder by person or persons unknown. Kemp then said that it was now up to the police to shed further light on the mystery and alluded to the many unsolved mysteries there had been in recent times. And that is all that is known of the matter.

We can only speculate about what happened. William Cliff seems to have been an inoffensive man, though one who liked a drink, which he could not hold. Why anyone should want to kill him is unknown. Did his brother have a long-standing grudge against him? Did the man who was fired hate him with such ferocity that he murdered him? Both seem very unlikely, given the information available. Who was the man seen with William outside the Anchor? Probably it was Walding, who later had a drink with him in the Red Cow, but whose movements thereafter seem accounted for. Did William know his assailant? Certainly the ferocity of the attack suggests either some deep personal hatred or that the killer had psychopathic tendencies. These questions will never be satisfactorily answered.

CHAPTER 16

The Uxbridge Gas Chamber, 1906

The gas was overwhelming in that room.

I n the early afternoon of Monday 18 June 1906 there came a strange letter for the Uxbridge police. Consisting of six folios, it was as rambling as it was long. It had been forwarded from Messrs Idris & Co., mineral water manufacturers, of London and it concerned one Edward Montague Williams, who had been employed by them as one of their salesmen for over two years. It said that he had murdered his family and before they received the letter he would already be dead. A local newspaper made a comparison with the Denham murder (chronicled in this book in Chapter 11).

PS Pengelly and PC Penfold cycled to the Williams's house. This was a detached villa, West View Cottage, which was on the junction of Ickenham Road (now Honeycroft Hill) and Park Road, not far from the Common and the sub post office. Finding the front door locked, the two officers entered through

Windsor Road, Uxbridge, c. 1930. Author's collection

a window. At once they could smell strong gas fumes, but the place itself was quiet. A quick search of the lower floor revealed nothing. They went upstairs and forced the bedroom door open. It was then that the most pungent odour of gas was experienced.

More shocking though, was the sight of four motionless bodies. Williams was lying on the bed, head downwards. He was, however, only unconscious. The other three were dead. His wife, Annie, 30, and the two children, Edward Montague, 3, and Charles Augustus, 18 months, had had their mouths covered with wadding, which had been soaked in chloroform. The cause of death was obvious, even without the smell. The gas fittings had been removed and a cut had been made in the pipe below the bracket. All means of ventilation had been blocked up so that the room was an airtight compartment.

Two policemen joined their colleagues and medical aid was summoned. Before Dr Ambrose Charpentier, of the High Street, and the divisional police surgeon arrived with Dr Walker, air was admitted into the once deadly chamber. Using oxygen and other attempts at resuscitation, they managed to revive Williams, at least in part. At 8 he was taken to the Union Infirmary in the police ambulance. Senior police officers arrived, as did a number of sightseers. The latter did not leave until the three corpses were removed to the mortuary. A macabre touch was that the foot of the youngest boy was sticking out of the vehicle when it left the house. The premises were then guarded by the police.

On the following day a post-mortem was performed on the three bodies. Relatives were allowed into the house under police supervision. The inquest was held at the Public Rooms in Uxbridge on Thursday. Reginald Kemp, deputy county coroner, presided. After the jurymen had seen the bodies, Kemp told them of the circumstances surrounding their discovery. He hoped that Williams would be soon recovered sufficiently to be able to give evidence before them. The only witness called was Mrs Augusta Julia Williams, the octogenarian mother of Williams. She had not seen the family since Easter, so could say little except that they seemed to be in good health then. One juror suggested that there should be a coroner's court in Uxbridge, but Kemp reminded them that, if there were, the rates would have to increase. However, he promised he would raise it with the county council. The court then adjourned until 6 July, to await further evidence.

Speculation surrounded Williams himself. He was aged 48 and was known to friends as 'Monte'. He had previously worked as a comedian in America and elsewhere in the world. Annie was his second wife and he had a grown-up daughter from his first marriage. The family had only lived locally for about eighteen months, having resided in Regent's Park previously. They were well liked and respected. He seemed contented and he and his wife were often seen in their garden, happily working together in the evening. Rather unconventionally, he worked in the garden without his waistcoat and with his shirt sleeves rolled up. He was handy about the house, and repaired his children's shoes. He also bred poultry. On the Sunday, it being a warm day, they had gone out for a drive to Ruislip and Eastcote, and his friends seemed to think he was his usual genial self. Although he was a regular at the Gardeners' Arms, just around the corner, he was not a heavy drinker.

Yet there were indications in the days leading up to the tragedy that all was not well. George Hamilton, an agent to the Anglo-Bavarian Brewery Co., and a friend of Williams, had talked to him on the previous Saturday. He recalled:

The Gardeners' Arms, 2007. Author's collection

He did not seem to be in his usual health. One had only to be in his company for a few minutes to know what an entertaining personality he possessed. He had for years been on the stage previous to holding his present position. He had travelled the States, and in fact been over all the world. He was a comedian of exceptional talent.

Furthermore, on the previous Friday, Williams had been paying his bills with various local tradesmen (at this time it was common for shopkeepers to allow their regular customers credit). Mr Kew, a butcher of Windsor Street, recalled that Williams settled his account and ordered a piece of beef for Sunday. On the following day Williams returned to the same shop and wanted to settle his account; apparently he had forgotten he had already done so. Kew thought the behaviour odd but Williams would only say: 'We are only a small family, and do not want to run any more accounts.' Williams also told the milkman not to call again and had paid Mrs Burroughs, from whom they were renting the house, all the rent that was due.

Williams had been to the local pub after the Sunday drive. Regulars there recalled that he had remarked that he might not be seen there again. Yet it was thought that this only meant that he was on bad terms with his boss and might be leaving the district.

The reason for the murders and suicide would never be known. Williams died at 11 am on 22 June. The following day saw the funeral of his wife and boys. They were buried at Hillingdon Cemetery. Many people attended the event or lined the route. Mrs Williams attended, supported by Detective Inspector Pollard. Many visited the grave and the house on the Sunday. On the following day the inquest was resumed, but just so that Williams's body could be identified and the coroner could issue a burial order. Williams was duly buried next to his family – another well attended event, though it was not as popular as the previous occasion.

On 6 July, the inquest was completed. There was little to say, except that Williams had killed his family during their sleep on the night of 17 June, then had attempted to kill himself.

Dr Lock presented the medical evidence. He said that when he had seen Williams he had been in a comatose condition, but that recovery did seem possible. Acute inflammation of the lungs, caused by morphia and gas poisoning, had been the cause. There were signs that Williams had injected himself in the chest with morphia and this would have affected his mind. Dr Charpentier said that Williams must have applied morphine to the others, and then chloroformed them. Morphia is tasteless, so it could have been applied to the children easily. It was possible that Annie might have taken it willingly.

The question was asked whether Williams had had money troubles or had been in difficulties with his employers. The agreement that he had signed with his employers was potentially very much in their favour, not his, and his mother had tried to persuade him not to sign it. However, Williams had not blamed his bosses when he wrote the lengthy message to them. In fact, he thanked them for their kindness towards him.

Sir Thomas Stevenson (1838–1908), who was an expert in poisons employed by the Home Office, spoke next. He said that there was three-quarters of a grain of morphia in Annie's body, half a grain in the older child and a third of a grain in the youngest. He suggested that Williams might have calculated the amount needed exactly. He concurred with his colleagues as to the cause of the deaths.

Kemp summed up. He believed that it was a very simple case of murder followed by suicide. He said that Williams had a morbid turn of mind and read books about toxicology. He added that he had money worries and was troubled by his wife's health. Apparently Williams had attempted suicide fifteen years previously. He was clearly unsound in mind on the fatal night.

Williams had been preparing the way for his actions. He had paid off the tradesmen and his landlady. He had taken the family for a final day out. Then he had told his friends in the pub that they would not see him there again. That night he proceeded to kill his family and then himself, beginning with chloroform he had bought previously. He had even sent a letter to his employers to tell them about it. He was a troubled man – the former comedian who now became the most tragic of figures. His exact motives are unknown, but Kemp's assessment seems likely enough.

CHAPTER 17

Disappearance at Yiewsley, 1933

If the boy's body is in that dump, it would be almost impossible to recognise any of it by now.

After 1906, there had not been a murder in this district for over a quarter of a century, despite the rapid increase in population, a happy situation that has never happened since. Even though the 1920s were noted as an era when crime was low, that around Uxbridge was exceptionally so. Therefore this case probably came as a shock. Most murder cases feature a corpse. This one, assuming it did feature a violent death, did not.

Mr Thomas and Mrs Olive Davidson were estranged. Their son, John, aged 7, was living with his mother in the Homeway, Hanwell. On Thursday, 14 December 1933, he left home for Hobbayne Infants' School, Hanwell, as usual. He never returned. His mother said, 'Since that day I have never set eyes on him or heard a word concerning his whereabouts from anyone. I have not heard from anyone who has seen him or anything like him since that last day at school.'

The investigation does not seem to have developed until the summer of the following year. The police kept telling Mrs Davidson to be patient. She said, 'How can I be patient?' Her son had attended a number of schools, because the family moved about. He had no firm friends at school. Yet he was bright, being able to read, write, tell the time, was quick, intelligent and mischievous. He easily made friends and knew his way about. His mother had two theories which might account for his disappearance, but did not hold out much hope that either was correct.

The first was:

Those things about the child made me think at one time that perhaps someone had taken a fancy to him, and had just taken him away and adopted him, but now I cannot think that anyone would be so callous as that. They must know, if that has happened, that the boy has parents somewhere.

The other was:

Then again I thought that perhaps friends of our family had found him somewhere, and were looking after him, but now I cannot think that that is so, because after all the fresh publicity, they would surely have communicated with the police.

Mrs Davidson, though only 28 years old, had a lined, sorrowful face. She was living in rooms under an assumed name, in Greenford Avenue, and even her friends did not know her new identity, seeing no one but her parents, who lived in West Ealing, where she was born. She just wanted some definite news, even if it were bad. She was not optimistic, saying, 'What can I say? Until lately, I used to think that I must see my boy again. I didn't think such things as this could happen. But now, after seven months, what can I think?

Yiewsley rubbish dump and canal, c. 1930. Philip Sherwood's collection

Some instinct seems to tell me now that I may never see my boy again.'

In June, attention focused on a rubbish dump in Yiewsley. The dump covered about nine acres and was full of old bedsteads, rotting paper, motor tyres, tin cans and other rubbish, and was about ten to twelve feet high. The refuse mostly came from London. Flies hovered about and people scavenged on it. It attracted attention because of a statement made by Davidson, now a prisoner in Pentonville, who was taken there by the police for the express purpose of locating the missing boy, who was now presumed to be dead. Davidson claimed the boy had been drowned in the canal and then buried in the dump. Furthermore, a dramatic statement was made by a Mr Amer, who lived at Lawn Cottages, and ran a piggery near the refuse dump at Yiewsley. Amer had seen a man and a boy there late the previous year.

Amer said, 'In October last year my boy asked me if a man could sleep in my pig sty. The man had been sleeping out on the dump at nights for several months.' The man told him that he would pay for shelter by helping with the pigs. At first Amer was reluctant as he could not pay any money, but the man proved to be a good worker and clean in his habits, so stayed for some time, especially as the weather was becoming colder for anyone staying out of doors at night.

The most important piece of news that Amer could impart was this:

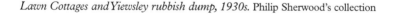

Lawn Cottages and Yiewsley rubbish dump, 1930s. Philip Sherwood's collection

On the Thursday before Christmas he brought along a boy to sleep the night. I never saw the boy again. As it happened, I told the man he had better clear off. He went and that was the last I saw of him.

If the boy had been killed nearby and disposed of in the dump then, despite the searches made there by locals, the portents of finding the body were poor, as Amer continued:

They seem to have given it up as a bad job now. If the boy's body is in that dump, it would be almost impossible to recognise any of it by now. You can see, it's like a furnace.

The police had also had been given permission to dig up part of the dump – that section which was next to the canal. This was marked off by stakes. Sir Bernard Spilsbury (1877–1947), famed Home Office pathologist, investigated the site and gave the gloomy opinion that if the boy had been buried there, several months before, it would be impossible to locate any recognizable remains.

Appeals were made by the BBC to anyone who had seen the boy in the last few months. It was thought that he might still have been alive in March. A number of people came forward to Inspector Greenacres of the Ealing police, who was in charge of the investigation. However, the information they had was so vague as to not be at all helpful. It was believed that he was cared for by a married couple in Hayes on 22–24 December. The couple in question were asked to come forward as soon as possible. However, it transpired that he was taken away by Thomas Davidson, his father.

On 27 August, at the Uxbridge Magistrates' Court, Davidson was charged with the murder of the lad. He confessed to the court:

I took him out of the water and laid him on the bank. I tried to pump water out of his stomach. It was hopeless … When I jumped into the canal it was my intention to do away with both of us.

Mr Clayton, in opening the case, told those assembled, that the Davidsons had not been getting on well together for some time and had been living apart. Davidson had removed his son from his home, promising to the landlady, Mrs Clack, to return him, but he never did. On the following day he told her that the boy had been injured in an accident, which, of course, was untrue. Davidson and his son arrived at the dump at 22 December, according to Amer. Two days later there was a conversation, which had been hitherto unknown.

The two men talked about breakfast on 24 December. Davidson said he didn't want any, and when Amer asked why, Davidson said, 'Jackie is dead'.

- Did he get knocked down by a motor car or something?
- No, he was following me across the dust [dump], and when he got to the dock, he fell in and was drowned.
- Jack, you did it.
- No.
- Did you make a mess at my place? Did you murder him up there?
- I took him away and put him in the dock and drowned him.

Amer had hitherto told no one of this conversation.

It was then also revealed that, thereafter, Davidson had been keeping up the pretence that his son was still living. He had claimed that in April he was keeping him away from his mother and that in July friends in Essex were looking after him. However, on 21 July he wrote to Greenacres:

Dear Sir – with reference to the enquiries as to the whereabouts of my son, Jackie, which has been going on for the last seven months – my son is dead. I killed him. I think it is best to make a clean breast of things and get things squared up. I do not intend to give any explanation as to why or how it happened in the letter or where he is buried. If my wife is brought along to see me, I will explain everything. He can be found in a very few hours. Otherwise you will dig for hours and find nothing. I do not expect her or wish her to see me on my own. She can be accompanied by anyone she wishes.

Davidson had explained to Greenacres, when he came to see him, that he had no further interest in life. He had persuaded his wife to come down to the dump on 19 December and she remained until 21 December. Then she left and, though he tried to see her again in order to make things up, had been unable to see her. So he returned to Jackie. He told how he had taken his son to the canal and they had jumped in. He climbed out, but his son was dead. Then he buried him on the dump.

Amer confirmed that he had let Davidson stay, and that he had seen him with the boy and also with his wife there. He was asked why he had not come forward earlier, after Davidson had confessed to killing his son. He said that he had considered it, but that he concluded that Davidson could not have done it, because he seemed so fond of the child. He added that he had no proof that Davidson was being truthful. Finally, he agreed that his duty had been to report him to the police.

The next witness was Norman Rose, a greengrocer of Allenby Road, Southall. Mrs Davidson had been staying at his house on 28 December when Davidson called for her at a quarter to midnight. He was not allowed to see her and left. It was then revealed what the relations between the parties were. Rose admitted that he and Mrs Davidson had been living together as man and wife for the past months, at least since early December 1933, when they had both resided in the same room in a house in the Homeway, Hanwell. He said he had hit Davidson after the latter had knocked his wife down. Rose denied that he had told Mrs Davidson to return to him or he would expose all he knew about her.

Relations between the Davidsons had, in fact, been poor for some time. Mrs Davidson showed the letter her husband had written to her on 30 July. He had written,

Thank God our innocent child will not grow up knowing what I have known ... Our child cried for three hours when

I said I would fetch him back to you ... I do not see any alternative to do, but to do what I have done to two unwanted ... I am looking forward to my end ... I have tried hard to do away with myself in the past, unfortunately I have failed.

Mrs Davidson agreed that her husband had been fond of their child, and said she had done her best to provide for him by going out to work. She denied her association with Rose had any bearing on the matter. She had left her son to be looked after by a variety of people while she worked. However, Inspector Greenacre claimed 'Certain evidence has come to my knowledge that the prisoner was not always kind to his son.'

The defending counsel said that there was no body and no proof that a murder had been committed. There was no charge that Davidson had to answer, therefore. However, the prosecution argued that it was possible for a murder charge to be brought even if there was no body, as had happened in a number of murders committed on the high seas. The letter to his wife and the statement made by Amer were corroborating evidence to Davidson's statement. The bench decided to send Davidson to the Old Bailey for trial.

Dr Hugh Grierson carried out an examination on Davidson to see whether he was sane or not. He wrote in his report, 'There is no family or personal history of any mental disorder. He says he had sunstroke in India in 1922 or 1923 ... While he has been here he has been normal in conduct and rational in conversation, and has shown no sign of insanity.' Therefore he was fit to plead.

On 18 September, Davidson was on trial for his life. He pleaded 'not guilty'. The prosecution outlined the facts of the case, of the disappearance of the boy, of Davidson's confession and the letter to his wife, admitting that he thought it better for their son that he was no longer alive to learn of his mother's wickedness. The court was told that father and son had jumped into the canal, but that Davidson had survived and removed his son's corpse from the canal.

Mrs Davidson testified that her husband had never shown any animosity towards their son. She added that he hated the people she chose to associate with. She no longer loved her husband, nor had for some time. She admitted that her husband still had feelings towards her. Ethel Clack related how Davidson removed his son and Amer recalled his conversations with him.

Davidson now stood in the box. He told how he was born in Cawston, Norfolk, in 1900 and his father was a farm labourer. Aged 14, he worked on the farm, but enlisted in the army in the following year and served until 1924. He then married, but from 1926 'his married life was a time of great unhappiness'. He recalled how he claimed his son was in tears about going back to his mother. But then he altered his former story:

> I left the boy by the hut while I went to get the sack. The time would be between 11 and 11.30 pm. Having found the sack I came back to where I had left the boy, but he was not there. I searched everywhere, using a torch. I found the boy in the water at 2.00 am on the following morning. The body was lying by the bank among some weeds. I took him out of the water and tried to pump the water out of his stomach. He showed no signs of life.

He then hid the body, but could not find it again, such was the rubbish which was later heaped upon it. He said he knew he should have reported this, but felt unable to do so, such was his panic. When asked, he denied that his confession and the story he told his wife were true. He had written the letter to his wife in order to try and persuade her to free herself of her association with Rose and added that he did not care what happened to him.

There was a lengthy summing up. Clearly Davidson felt no hatred towards his son. Much depended on what the jury believed. Was the confession true, or not? Confessions of crimes which the confessor had not committed were not unknown. But Davidson had undoubtedly made those statements. Why had he left the corpse near to the dump? He had later told Amer, but that was some time after. The judge clearly did not believe that Davidson's new version of events was true.

It only took the jury fifteen minutes to decide that Davidson was guilty of murder. He was sentenced to death. However, the solicitors for the defence lodged an appeal two days later, on the grounds that the evidence was insufficient and the judge had misdirected the jury. Three judges in the Court of Criminal Appeal heard this a few weeks later but did not think it necessary to overturn the original sentence. Finally, although Davidson was ready for execution, the Home Secretary granted a reprieve and so Davidson was given life imprisonment.

What exactly happened near the dump in Yiewsley is impossible to know. It is probable that the suicide/murder attempt was made, and that Davidson only changed his story after he had been in discussion with his lawyers.

CHAPTER 18

Murder without Motive? 1937

I went into the bedroom, switched on the electric light and saw Lily lying on the floor in a pool of blood.

By August 1937, petite, dark-haired and attractive Mrs Lilian Chamberlain had been only married a year. She worked as a barmaid at the Northwood Hotel and lived opposite her place of work in a flat on Green Lane. Ivan, her husband, was also in the catering trade, serving food on the railways. This meant that he was absent for a number of nights each week. She had gone home at 10.45 on the evening of 25 August, after chatting with customers.

She did not arrive at work at 9 as usual, though, on the following morning. Inquiries were soon made at the flat by Maurice Lammas, the hotel's handyman. He rang three times

Green Lane, Northwood, 1920s. Author's collection

3056. - SOLDIERS MEMORIAL AND GREEN LANE (Central), NORTHWOOD.

and received no reply. He then opened the door and made a horrific discovery. Her room was in disarray and there had clearly been a struggle there. But attention was focused on the unclothed body of Mrs Chamberlain, who had severe head injuries. She had been subject to a frenzied assault. Lammas recalled:

> When I opened the door I saw her body lying on the floor. She was lying on her back with the feet towards me and her arms outstretched. She was covered in blood from head to foot.

Lammas left the room and arrived at the police station at 10.05. He told PS George Shadbolt the news. Once the latter arrived on the scene, he called for Dr William Russell, who lived on the same street and arrived at 10.20. Shadbolt noted that there were a number of head wounds, probably caused by a heavy blunt instrument, such as a jemmy or a poker. The victim had been strangled, too. Death had occurred at least eight hours before. Sir Bernard Spilsbury later examined the corpse. He observed, 'In my opinion, the cause of death was strangulation by a ligature round the neck.'

Superintendent Yandell and his men were soon on the scene to look for clues and witnesses. Pieces of cloth, carpet and a small piece of wood were sent to the police laboratory at Hendon. Any article in the room on which there might be fingerprints was photographed and then removed. None of the neighbours in the flats could shed any light on the murder. No unusual noises had been heard that night.

However, information came from another source. It led, later that day, to the arrest of one John Rodgers, a 22-year-old barman, also of Northwood, at Golders Green. Detective Inspector Carson said 'I conveyed him to Northwood police station, where he made a statement which I took down in writing in the presence of Superintendent Yandell … He was cautioned. I read the statement to him and he signed it … When I read over the charge to him, he made no reply.'

The statement began with a summary of Rodgers's life history. It had certainly been an unlucky one. He was born in

Liverpool in 1916 and never knew his father. Much of his childhood was spent in an orphanage in Bristol and he never saw his mother after 1924. Leaving the orphanage aged 14, he drifted into crime. He was bound over for stealing from shops in 1930. A year later he was in trouble for theft yet again. This time he was sent to a borstal for three years.

In 1934 he began an unsettled life on the outskirts of London. He worked in post office sorting offices, hotels and pubs, having to leave once for embezzlement and drinking. He befriended one Irene Scott, a few years younger than himself, when employed in a hotel in Chorley Wood. At the beginning of 1937, he was employed as a barman in the Northwood Hotel. This was where he first met Mrs Chamberlain.

He then recounted his version of the events of the day of the murder and the one following. He had his usual afternoon off on the 25 August. He had taken a boat on the Ruislip reservoir (the Lido), then took a train to Rickmansworth. Here he visited two pubs, the Swan and the Coach and Horses, staying until almost 10. He played darts and chatted to acquaintances. Then he took a Green Line coach back to Northwood, arriving at just after 10. He did not seem particularly drunk, according to witnesses.

For some reason he decided to sleep by the gravel pits, instead of returning to the hotel. He felt unwell due to the

Ruislip reservoir/lido, c. 1915. Author's collection

alcohol. However he changed his mind, as he said: 'I was thinking of sleeping rough, but could not make myself comfortable, so thought I would go to Lily's flat, and see if she and her husband could put me up.' It was now too late to return to the hotel. Entering the flats by a ground-floor window, he went to the first floor, where the Chamberlains' flat was and he told the police:

> I then shouted 'Ivan', which is the name of Lily's husband and there was no reply, but I heard groans and then went upstairs. The bedroom door was ajar and the place was in darkness, but I lighted matches on the way up. I went into the bedroom, switched on the electric light and saw Lily lying on the floor in a pool of blood, badly knocked about. Her eyes seemed to be open and she said, in a funny sort of way, almost frowning it, 'Oh John, Oh John.'

He then tried to move her onto the bed, but without success. In doing so, his clothes became covered in blood. He removed them and put on some of her husband's clothes. When asked why, if this account was true, he did not try and summon help, he replied, 'When I left the flat I was scared and it did not occur to me to go to the hotel or to the police station.' He disposed of his bloodstained coat and trousers near a stream.

Instead, Rodgers decided he wanted to leave Northwood, so went to the railway station and asked the booking clerk, one Harold Sawyer, when the next train was. It was now 12.50 pm. Sawyer told him that the last train to Rickmansworth had left at five to midnight, but that there was a train to Watford due shortly. After some indecision, Rodgers decided to walk. Sawyer later stated, 'He was perfectly ordinary and normal as far as I observed. He spoke clearly and distinctly without any sign of distress.' No sign then of the panic which Rodgers later claimed that he was in.

On his nocturnal walk, Rodgers encountered two policemen, who asked who he was and 'Why are you hanging about these shops here?' Rodgers said 'I work at the Northwood Hotel. I came home late and cannot get in, so I am walking about.' He could prove his identity and so they let him on his way.

Eventually he arrived at Harrow and took the train from there to Liverpool Street station. He spent the day at Southend, where he bought some new clothes, ate and briefly spoke to a girl. Returning to Liverpool Street station, he took a train to Golders Green. It was there that he was recognized, by William Gardiner, a bus conductor, who knew the police were looking for Rodgers, and who also knew the wanted man.

He was remanded at Uxbridge Magistrates' Court for a week on the charge of murder. No members of the public were present during the hearing and his presence there had been kept a secret. Rodgers 'was a short figure, with dark hair brushed straight back, and he was dressed in a sports jacket and open neck shirt'. Although he was told that he could ask questions of the inspector, he was advised not to without legal representation. Rodgers was allowed to have the services of Mr Johnson, a Hayes solicitor. 'What should I want legal aid for?' asked the accused man. Mr Robbins, the magistrate replied, 'You are on the most serious charge that a man can be charged with, and the law provides for your defence. Would you like Mr Johnson to defend you?' Rodgers agreed that he would. He was then sent down to appear at the court in the following week.

Northwood Police Station, 2007. Author's collection

There are conflicting statements about his relations with Lilian. Rodgers claimed a friendship with her, but admitted he had only been into her flat once, having been asked by her to take a photograph of her in her bathing costume, a photograph which he did not have a copy of. Tessie O'Connor said that Rodgers was friendly with everyone, and not especially so with Mrs Chamberlain. One witness said that Rodgers had once used bad language towards Mrs Chamberlain. A completely different interpretation was given by a regular at the pub, Norman Reed, in a letter to the police of 1 September. He recounted a conversation he had had in the bar with the late barmaid after the latter shivered:

- What's the matter, cold?
- No; but I always shiver when that man comes near.
- Whom? Maurice?
- No, not Maurice. That man from the lower bar, I always shiver when he comes near me. I hate going into the lower bar while he is there.
- Why?
- I don't quite know. I think it is the way he looks at me. He frightens me.

Reed added that the victim was 'a woman of the highest integrity, and the soul of honour', and that 'Whether this man is the actual murderer or not, I do not of course know, but I can assure you that Mrs Chamberlain had a genuine fear.' The man in question, of course, was Rodgers.

Rodgers was sent to prison to await trial. Dr Hugh Grierson examined him. According to him, 'he has been well-behaved, has conversed normally and rationally. Examination has not revealed any evidence of any mental disorder.' Therefore, Rodgers was deemed sane and fit to plead in court. The trial could proceed.

On 24 September, another piece of physical evidence appeared to come to light. George Barry, a labourer employed by the council, was emptying the rubbish bins near to the gravel pits in Rickmansworth Road. These had not been emptied for two months. In one he found a long chisel. He took this to the police and it was later identified by Lammas as being one which was normally kept in the hotel's cellar, which was just off the premises. It had been missing since at least 26 August. Was this, then, the murder weapon? Yet, on closer examination, though there were rust stains on its end, no traces of blood could be detected. They may have been wiped off, and a flannel smeared with blood was also located.

The case came up at the Old Bailey on 18 October, nearly two months after the murder had been committed. Messrs McClure and Christmas Humphreys were prosecuting. They recounted Rodgers's movements on the day before and after the murder. McClure did not suggest that Rodgers entered the flat with murder on his mind, and the weapon he had was only initially meant as a tool to aid his entering the place. Spilsbury elaborated on the nature of the injuries suffered by the victim, He said that the shoulder straps of Mrs Chamberlain's own nightdress might have been used. They could have been drawn tightly around her neck by Rodgers's hands. This would have caused death within five minutes. The other wounds were caused before she had been strangled, possibly whilst she was on the floor, and would have rendered her unconscious, perhaps for ten minutes. They did not kill her, but even if strangulation had not occurred, might have proved fatal nonetheless.

When the accused was placed in the box, he did not make a favourable impression. He gave his version of the events; namely that he saw the battered body of Mrs Chamberlain, then panicked. When pressed, he said that he could have gone for help. McClure asked him why he did not. Rodgers then made the revealing comment, 'With me it is self first, self last and self always.' He was also pressed to admit, though he claimed he was flustered, that he had carefully changed clothes and taken away the bloody ones, all while Mrs Chamberlain lay dying nearby.

Mr St John Hutchinson, defending, asked the jury not to be prejudiced by the 'unpleasant and callousness of the defendant'. The jury took two hours to deliberate over Rodgers's fate. They found him guilty, but asked that mercy be shown on account of his youth. The judge then addressed

Rodgers, 'The jury have rightly found that you have been guilty of this most brutal murder.' Rodgers, who had smiled on entering the dock, flushed when he heard the sentence. When motioned by the warders to leave, he turned smartly, slapped the pockets of his jacket and ran down the steps out of sight. Rodgers attempted to gain a reprieve from the death sentence. None was given. He was hanged at Pentonville Prison on 19 November.

The only puzzling question is that of motive. The judge had said that, although none could be found, that was not necessary in order to find someone guilty. When Rodgers entered the Chamberlains' flat he discovered, if he did not already know it, that only Mrs Chamberlain was there, alone and vulnerable. Had her husband been there, the story would have been very different. Clearly robbery was not the motive as no money or jewellery was searched for nor taken. Sex was not the motive, either. Nor was it a case of revenge or passion. One possibility was that this hitherto petty criminal felt angry or frustrated and this led to murder. It was almost certainly not premeditated, but a spur of the moment decision which was to prove fatal for them both.

CHAPTER 19

The Assailant who Never was, 1938

*You know who we are. I am going to take you into custody
and charge you with the wilful murder of your wife …*

In 1938, Sidney George Paul was a 46-year-old
unemployed salesman, who lived with his Belgian
wife, Claire, aged 39, in a house in Rosebury Vale,
Ruislip. Paul had been born in Battersea, but emigrated to
Australia when he was 18. During the First World War, he
served in the Fifth Field Ambulance Force. He married Claire
in 1920 and between 1922 and 1930 they had had four
children. They lived in Belgium and the Belgian Congo for
many years and lived well – a witness recalled that they
'deprived themselves of nothing, lived on a large scale'. Then,
in January 1938, they returned to England, leaving the two
elder children (Nancy, 16, and Marie, 17) at school in
Belgium, and bought a house in Ruislip, worth £1,100. Few
people nearby knew much about them; perhaps in part
because Claire could speak very little English, though her
husband spoke four languages.

It seemed to be a happy marriage. In the summer of 1938
they had holidayed in Coxyde and someone recalled, 'I noticed
nothing abnormal, they even seemed to get on well together …
appeared to live on good terms and always in good humour.'

Misfortune first struck early one Sunday morning in May.
They were awakened by neighbours, telling them that their
house was on fire. They escaped in their pyjamas using a
ladder thoughtfully provided by the neighbours. Although the
fire only destroyed the contents of one room, these included
80 oil paintings, a 1760 violin, some priceless glass, ivory and
the luggage of their two elder children.

Yet an even worse tragedy was to strike the family. Oddly
enough, they had been to a concert in London on the previous

night and they had also visited the same concert hall on the night before the fire in May. A friend remarked 'When they returned home, they remarked their previous visit to the same hall, and laughingly wondered if any ill-luck would follow.' It was to be far worse. On the morning of Sunday 16 October 1938, the Pauls' children had left home to attend mass. Paul had gone out for some cigarettes. It was about 8 o'clock.

He later related, on returning home, that he and his wife had some tea. She then went downstairs, to wash the floor of the verandah. Next he heard a sound:

I heard a noise like somebody walking about in the bedroom upstairs and opening the wardrobe doors. I was then in the w.c., which is near the bedroom on the same floor. I then heard my wife scream and saw my wife lying on the verandah at the rear of the house. I went through the kitchen which leads on to the verandah. The verandah door was open. The verandah door leads into the garden and I went through I felt a bang on my head from the side and I fell down.

I got another crack as I was lying on the floor. I got up and saw a man, clean shaven with black hair with a black cap on and blue jacket, rubber boots on and rubber gloves. He has a scar on the right cheek, white and vivid, a well-built man of about 40 ... I caught hold of his coat in the front. The man struck me again. I grappled with him, and he got away.

Paul rushed out into the street and knocked on the door of Mrs Emily Woolley's house, where a policeman lodged. Looking out of the window, she saw Paul with blood streaming down his face. He said, 'Come quickly, there's a man in my house' and then returned to his own house. Other neighbours recalled him bemoaning, 'My poor wife! She's going to die; she's going to die!' and 'whatever will the children do without her?' Dr McCarthy was called for, followed by PC Carlin. The latter recalled that Paul was in a very excitable state, saying 'There he is again. He will get me if you don't watch him.' Paul gave him the button he had taken from his assailant's coat.

Rosebury Vale, Ruislip, 2007. Author's collection

Mrs Paul was found lying on the verandah floor, on her stomach. Her head lay in a pool of blood. She was still breathing, but only just. The bedroom above was in a state of disarray. The wardrobe's door was half-open.

The two injured people were sent to Hillingdon Hospital where, later that day, Claire died of her injuries, with detectives and a priest by her bedside. She never regained consciousness. Her husband had lesser injuries and made a quick recovery, being able to leave on the same day.

The police investigation began. They first looked for physical clues in and around the Pauls' house. An axe was found, wrapped in a cloth and partially hidden. Both were wet. There was a bloodstain on its haft. There was also a pail with discoloured water. This turned out to be blood. Marks were found on the wardrobe which had been forced in order to get at the £150, in one pound notes, which had been there, according to Paul. But the marks appeared to have been made when the door was already open. Detectives guarded the house and Sir Bernard Spilsbury was called in as well as officers from Scotland Yard.

Paul gave the police a description of the attacker and on the day following the murder, the police issued this:

Age 30 to 35; 6 feet tall, heavy build; pale complexion, white scar $^3/_4$ inch long and $^1/_4$ inch wide in the centre of the right cheek; clean shaven; dark hair; was dressed in a dark blue or black cloth cap, dark blue suit, dark blue or black muffler, rubber boots and a white tab in front at the top.

None of the Pauls' neighbours had anything important to report about the morning of the murder. Herbert Valey, a neighbour, recalled that at about 7.30–7.45, he had seen two of the children leave the house. Milkmen, delivering their wares between 6 and 7, had seen nothing suspicious. Nor had Brian Trafford, a paper boy. Inspector Ferrier noted, 'It is appreciated that this was a wet Sunday morning and as the hour is generally considered to be early for rising on a Sunday, there would be few people about.'

Who was the strange assailant? Paul recalled that his attacker wore pink gloves. Mrs Cooper, a neighbour, said that she had seen someone's hands on Paul, but couldn't describe them or say if they belonged to a man or a woman. There were footprints in the RAF sports field behind the house. Mr Gelder of Bradford recalled seeing a man who fitted the killer's description at Bridlington in September, and others thought they saw a similar man at Erith. Unfortunately, their descriptions were vague and would have fitted hundreds of men. The footprints were of no use because a rugby match had been played on the field, and in any case the back fence was secure and it did not seem anyone had crossed it.

Superintendent Martin was unconvinced by Paul's story. He later wrote:

The first thing which aroused the officers' suspicions was the fact that Paul discharged himself from hospital the same day. This fact, combined with the relatively light injuries Paul had received set the officers on a certain line of enquiry, but in this direction, they were repulsed on every occasion, as enquiries showed that Paul and his wife were looked on as a devoted and ideal couple.

The police believed that Paul's story was a pack of lies. The injuries on his head could have been self-inflicted by a razor. There was little sign that there had been an intruder. If there had, how had he unerringly gone to the wardrobe in which money was allegedly concealed?

Had this money even ever existed? Paul's finances were investigated. He was found to be heavily in debt and his wife was pregnant. He had many debts; being 25s in arrears for a water-softening device, owed £2 2s 8d to the electricity company, £1 2s 1d for rates, 2 guineas for insurance and owed a builder £5. He had tried to borrow £25 from Father Sutton, his Catholic priest. Paul had asked at the Ruislip branch of the Royal British Legion for work. Paul suffered from insomnia and it was noted that he had a cut on his wrist – an indication of an attempt at suicide?

Ferrier concluded:

> This state of affairs, together with the fact that he was in arrears with rent due to the mortgages and that his wife is pregnant, is sufficient in my opinion to unsettle the state of his mind and provide a motive for murder, and the whole thing probably arose out of a quarrel with his wife on Sunday morning, 16th October 1938, respecting these matters.

Martin noted 'all the vital evidence forthcoming was circumstantial, and only obtained through the painstaking and careful manner in which the case was conducted'.

On Wednesday 19 October, Ferrier and Chief Inspector Burt went to visit Paul at his house, where he was playing with his children. Ferrier said to the widower, 'You know who we are. I am going to take you into custody and charge you with the wilful murder of your wife … ' Paul interrupted him: 'I didn't do it. I didn't do it.' Ferrier continued, '… your wife Claire Paul on 16 October, caused by striking her on the head with a instrument'. Paul replied, 'It is not right. It cannot be right.' Paul was taken to Ruislip Police Station, was charged and cautioned. He continued to appear to be in a state of shock, saying 'Can I go down and see Claire again?' and 'It isn't right. I don't know why you say it.' Paul appeared before Uxbridge Magistrates' Court and then was sent to Brixton prison to await trial.

At the inquest, Henry Paul, Paul's brother, formally identified the corpse. He added that she was a healthy woman. Spilsbury had made a post-mortem examination on 18 October and reported, 'The cause of death … was a fracture of the skull and an injury to the brain due to blows from some heavy cutting instrument.' This was undoubtedly the axe which had been found. Claire was buried on 25 October after a ceremony at Ruislip Catholic Church. There were few onlookers and few attended the funeral.

Paul made his next appearance before the magistrates on 3 November. Having been brought from prison in a police car, he was smartly dressed and protested his innocence. The first witness was Mr Cooper. He said he had, from his bedroom window, a view of the verandah where the murder had been committed. He had seen Paul stoop over his wife. He had picked something up and appeared to be striking something – or someone – with it. Cooper had seen no third person, as suggested by Paul. It was also asked how could the mysterious intruder have found the money from the wardrobe? Given that the Pauls were short of money, did this cash even ever exist? Why was the murder weapon carefully washed and then hidden? Similar buttons to the one that Paul alleged he tore from the attacker were found in a tin in the house. Paul said his wounds had been inflicted when the attacker struck his head on the wall, but this was impossible, whereas it was possible that they had been self-inflicted by a safety razor.

Spilsbury, after describing the victim's injuries, added that she was pregnant. It is interesting to note that this fact did not attract any particular sense of outrage or horror – that the killer had not only murdered Mrs Paul, but also her unborn baby too. It was, in some ways, a less sensitive age.

Paul's financial affairs were then examined. They were certainly dire. The Pauls only had 4 pence in their bank account. His sister, Mrs Goadby, who lived in Wembley, had loaned the family £150 in February, which had yet to be repaid. She wondered if Mrs Paul had her own reserve of cash unbeknown to her husband and whether this might have been kept upstairs in the wardrobe. If this is correct, then perhaps the money was indeed missing, but even so, it might have been concealed elsewhere by the cash-strapped Paul. Paul was committed for trial later that month at the Old Bailey.

On 28 November the three-day trial began at the Old Bailey. Mr McClure, for the prosecution, argued: 'this is a sad story, a story you may have read the like of, where a breaking point is reached in someone's experience, where everything is pressing, and things become too hard ... and it sometimes ends in murder or suicide of two people'. Paul was in desperate financial straits. It was alleged that an additional motive was Mrs Paul's pregnancy and the additional financial burden that an extra child would put on Paul's already desperate situation. Therefore he killed his wife and faked a murder and robbery. There was no evidence that anyone had broken in and no one else had clearly seen the alleged intruder.

On 30 November Mr Eastwood spoke for the defence. He told the court that the Pauls were a happy couple and there was no motive for the cold-blooded murder. Paul said he had no objection to his wife having another child and denied he inflicted any injuries on himself. He said he had no reason to kill his wife, to whom he was devoted. He claimed that his wife had talked about the money in the wardrobe to others, so a burglar might know where it was. Dr Arnott said the head injuries showed evidence of some violence being used and, whilst they could have been made by Paul, he thought it was unlikely. Mrs Cooper said she did see an intruder:

She then heard a second noise and thought it was Mr Paul groaning. She got out of bed and looking through the bedroom window again, saw Mr Paul sitting on the ground. His head was bleeding very much all over his face. His hands were slightly up and there was someone in dark clothes leaning over him, with their hands on his shoulders. Mr Paul was pushing the person away.

She was unsure whether the other person was male or female.

Yet on 1 December, after fifty minutes of debate, the jury returned and Paul was found guilty and sentenced to death, to be carried out on 18 December. Two weeks later, this was commuted to life imprisonment. It seems highly probable that Paul was guilty. If he was the loving husband as claimed, then why did he choose to kill his wife in such a shocking and brutal fashion? He appears, rather, to have been a selfish man, who put his financial interests first, and a not very clever one, in staging a faked robbery by a man whose existence was impossible to verify. If £150 was really stolen, then why had Paul not used it previously to help pay off his debts? None of his story made any sense and none could be verified. He had means, motive and opportunity. The only doubt must be in Mrs Cooper's statement, which conflicts with that of her husband's, as he seemed to suggest that Paul was the killer whilst her statement suggested the direct opposite.

CHAPTER 20

Murder by Person or Persons Unknown, 1954

She was alone and I cannot recall anyone else being in the vicinity.

On the morning of Wednesday 15 September 1954 there was a rumour circulating in South Ruislip that a child had been murdered. Police were active around the junction of Angus Drive and Victoria Road. Polling booths were used to screen the site from passersby. As the day progressed, it was said that the victim was a young woman. This was the truth.

In 1954 Miss Jean Mary Townsend was a 21-year-old dress designer of the women's department of a Leicester Square firm of theatrical and film costumiers. She was the only child of Reginald Townsend, a telephone engineer, and his wife, who also worked, and lived with them in their house at Bempton Drive, Ruislip Gardens. She had previously attended Lady Bankes' School, Ruislip Manor, and then attended Ealing Technical College from the age of 11. The Townsends were respected locally. Mr C J Young said 'Jean was a nice girl and always minded her own business.' Peter Kendon remarked, 'Jean was shy and reserved.' It was said she was 'a young woman of very respectable reputation'. Most of her interests, though, lay outside Ruislip and were concerned with the arts. Although her current job involved modelling costumes, she also came into contact with stars of the stage and screen.

She had a meal with her parents on the evening of Tuesday 14 September 1954. Then she went into the West End to attend a party in The Londoner Club, Irving Street (she was an honorary member), presumably using the Central Line tube as transport. She was involved with the Pyramid Club

Bempton Drive, Ruislip, 2007. Author's collection

craze, in which people are invited to a party and pay the host a small fee. They must then introduce new members to the circle, who give them money to give to the original host. Then the pyramid's base grows and in theory everyone gains financially, as long as the numbers involved swell. Paul Clay, the host recalled, 'Jean was in a wonderful mood.'

After the party she went alone to Oxford Circus tube station and took the last train home, alighting at South Ruislip station. Edgar Philips, a porter there, recalled that she arrived at about 11.45. He had seen her many times before over the past three years, and she had a weekly season ticket. The street lights were all extinguished at midnight. Some of her walk home would have been in the dark. She never arrived.

Her father later recalled:

She did not say what time she would return home. We expected her back between 11pm and midnight. She did not come back and I left the house at 8am the next day to telephone her place of business. I was not worried about her although it was unusual for her to be away for a night. She had friends in town with whom she might have stayed.

Junction of Victoria Road and Angus Grove, Ruislip, 2007. Author's collection

On the morning of the following day, at about 7, Charles Keys, a printer, found her corpse in the long grass a few feet from a footpath at the junction of Angus Drive and Victoria Road. This ground was on her direct route from the station to her home, about three-quarters of a mile away. He recalled:

> She was about five yards from the footway. She had no shoes or stockings on and her stockings were by her feet. A scarf was round her neck and she appeared to be dead. I telephoned Scotland Yard and waited for the police to arrive.

PC George Yate was driving a police car when a radio message told him to drive to the scene of the crime. He saw the body, talked to Keys and contacted his superiors and a doctor. Dr Maurice Edmund from Northwood arrived at ten to eight and examined the body, declaring life to be extinct. Dr Nickolls, a police doctor, who had recently taken part in the infamous Reginald Christie case, also examined the corpse and the area surrounding it. He noted that the knickers, stockings and shoes were near the corpse's feet, possibly dragged off when the body was moved to its present location. There was nothing that could help identify the killer, though.

Superintendent Robert Richardson was recalled from leave to take charge of the case. Miss Townsend's body was fully clothed, except for her shoes and a stocking, which were found with her handbag nearby. Death had been due to strangulation – Jean's black and gold scarf had been wound around her neck. The pathologist's examination indicated that death had taken place between 11.30 pm and 12.30 am. The grass near to the body had been flattened. There was no sign of sexual interference, though a contemporary crime writer speculated that there may have been an attempt at such.

Door-to-door questioning was used in all the houses in the two streets adjoining the murder site. The questions asked were 'Did you hear noise or sounds of a struggle?' and 'Did you hear a car stop during night time?'

Several people did come forward. Two days before the murder, Mr J O'Dell, a 26 year old employed at the American Embassy, had chased a man in his front garden who he thought might be a 'Peeping Tom'. He was wearing a brown jacket and light trousers. A more promising lead came from Miss Brenda Thompson, whose bedroom overlooked the murder location. She said she heard a woman cry for help at about the time of the murder. She added 'Five or six minutes later I hear two men arguing. One man spoke with an American or nasal twang. He sounded agitated.' Police thought that one man was trying to quieten his companion, but was now frightened to come forward, perhaps because of the other man. She pressed her face to the window, but could not see anyone.

There were a number of local reactions to the crime. One Walter Lack, a father of a teenage girl and a former army sergeant, organized vigilante patrols to ensure that the area was safe. He also appealed to the Ruislip Manor Residents' association for extra manpower. The police were said not to mind such volunteer help. Although the Residents' Association was not enthusiastic about Lack's proposals, they did suggest that the council keep one in three of the street lights on until 1 am.

Local women were frightened to walk in that part of Ruislip. A number reported their experiences in the locality. Violet

Ingram, aged 16, said that she had been pursued by a balding cyclist on the Thursday before the murder. She said 'He spoke with an accent, either Irish or Scottish.' Her sister Margaret recalled being approached by strangers in the Victoria Road area when she had been returning home from the station, 'But I have never been attacked.' Finally, their eldest sister, June, recalled that, on the Saturday before the killing, she was asked by a motorist to get into her car. The man had an American accent. This was only 20 yards from where Jean's corpse was later found. Other girls talked about having been attacked or about being accosted by motorists in the same locality. One said her assailant was a short man, wearing crepe shoes. A girl was accosted at nearby Pinner on 9 October by a man in his twenties with a high forehead. Mothers refused to allow their daughters to go out unaccompanied and girls banded together in groups of four or five if they intended leaving home after dark.

One theory was that perhaps a man from the nearby American Air Force base could have been involved – this was less than half a mile from the place where Jean's body had been found. This housed the Third United States Air Force and had been established in 1949. It was located at the south-eastern end of Victoria Road and bordered on Field End to the east and the railway line to the south (there is a large shopping estate there now). The site was expanded in 1951 and over 2,000 personnel were stationed there. Hundreds of dependants lived locally, too. Some Americans were troublesome. In early 1954, one American serviceman had been found guilty of drunken driving and killed a man; another American had been found guilty of other offences.

Yet officials there denied that they had been involved with police enquiries. Five American servicemen had been travelling on the last train back to South Ruislip, and they left before Jean did. They seemed to be behaving normally and were unable to help when questioned. Finally, an American spokesman said, 'Liaison with the British police is continuous. It does not stop and start with an emergency such as this.'

One early theory was that she could have been given a lift in a car, strangled there and then dragged out of it. Or she might have been attacked by someone lying in wait, perhaps with an accomplice.

Two men, aged about 24, had been seen on the spot where the murder had occurred on the evenings of 11 and 13 September. One was wearing a red or maroon wind-cheater. They were driving a sports car. A statement by Scotland Yard read 'Police would like to trace these two men, who, they believe, may be able to assist in their inquiries.'

Three other cars were sought. One was a red sports model, which had been seen on the night before the murder in the same vicinity. A saloon car was seen parked near to the scene of the crime on the night of the murder. The third car's driver came forward and was eliminated from police enquiries.

A number of other steps were taken by the police. Messages were flashed on local cinema screens to ask the public for any information they might have. Countrywide searches were made for the cars mentioned above. A young man with wavy hair, who caught a late night bus (the number 158) not far from the crime scene was sought, for he might have seen something. Apparently he alighted at Harrow Wealdstone. Two men in grey mackintoshes seen near the scene of the crime were sought, found and eliminated from enquiries. The South Ruislip ticket collector told police that he had seen Jean leave the station alone. A bloody shirt was handed into a local laundry, two days after the murder, but it provided no clue. Allegedly, the man who brought it in was in his twenties, had an American accent and a high forehead. Other women who had been attacked recently told the police of their experiences. One of these was an American. Police concluded that Jean did not know her attacker.

The inquest had begun at Ealing Town Hall in the week following the murder. Reginald Townsend formally identified his daughter. He wanted to have his daughter cremated. However, the coroner, Mr Broadbridge, would not allow this because proceedings were not yet complete. Dr Teare, a pathologist, announced that death had been due to strangulation by the victim's own scarf and had probably occurred before 12.30. Richardson asked for the inquest to be adjourned so that more information could be gathered, so it was.

South Ruislip tube station, 2007. Author's collection

The inquest took place at Ealing Town Hall on 19 October. Despite hundreds of people having been interviewed in the preceding weeks, no one had been identified as having been involved in the murder. A number of additional witnesses gave their evidence. Miss Patricia Kemp, a Greenford secretary, recalled seeing Jean at about 11.05 get onto the tube at Oxford Circus, but as Miss Kemp left at Greenford, had little more to report. John Smith, a Ruislip bank clerk, was being driven in a car by Captain John White of the American Air Force. They were driving near Victoria Road at about 10.45. He recalled:

> I saw a girl near the petrol station ... she was young and was wearing a whitish coat. She was walking along the road on our right. When I saw her the street lights were still on. She was alone and I cannot recall anyone else being in the vicinity. She was walking at an average pace as going about her own business.

Yet this could not have been Jean because she did not alight from the South Ruislip tube station until about 11.45.

Richardson said that it would have been possible for someone to have hidden in the two foot high grass in order to take his victim by surprise. This seemed likely, for there was no evidence of any struggle, either on the ground, or on Jean's body.

Mr Broadbridge, the coroner, could only note that 'lots of little clues turned up', but these proved to be worthless. He raised a couple of pertinent questions:

> The knowledge that has been gained has shown that there are some peculiar features in this case. They are very strange. The scarf was wound tightly round Miss Townsend's neck but none of her other clothing was disarranged in any other way except some of her underwear. There were no signs of a struggle. She was a well-built young woman of 21. One would have thought that had anyone tried to assault her, she would have defended herself. But not a mark was found on her beyond the injuries to her neck.

The jury could only return a verdict of 'murder by person or persons unknown'. A report in a local newspaper in 1971 about another woman murdered in South Ruislip made reference to this case, but declared it to be still unsolved. This part of Ruislip has sometimes been called 'Ruislip's murder mile'. Police investigations continued and information was still being collected as recently as 1982. It is unknown whether Jean had any enemies or had a boyfriend – her personal life seems a closed book. It seems probable that she was taken completely by surprise; probably by a man lying in wait for her – or by a woman. Or was she given a lift and then killed shortly afterwards, her body being dumped nearby? This sounds like a dangerous ploy for the killer. Whether the motive was personal or not is another question. It may have been sexual, as some of the girl's underwear had been removed. Was an American from the airbase involved? Possibly. An American accent was certainly heard by Brenda Thompson just after the scream. Unfortunately, as she did not see the killer, that does not lead us very far. Given the menace of the Cold War, it was important for the British government not to upset the American government, so it is possible that investigations among American servicemen might not have been pressed too far. The political situation was too sensitive. However, if this was so, it is odd that there was no reference to the matter in the Cabinet minutes of the time. Local opinion certainly thought an American serviceman was to blame, but it should be remembered that outsiders are often blamed, though not always wrongly, for crimes committed in any locality.

When the police file on the case is fully opened up in the distant future, we may know the truth, or at least have a far better idea of what the police actually thought was the truth. At time of writing the official line is that any public disclosure would prejudice any future investigation, although whether there is one, or will be, is unknown to the public. But since there has been no addition to the murder file since 1982 and, over half a century later, the killer is probably dead, it would appear that further inquiries are improbable. Until this attitude and time pass, the case is as mysterious now as it was in October 1954.

CHAPTER 21

Spies in Suburbia, 1961

the little suburban house was the communication centre
of this spy ring.

After the Second World War, conflict continued but became less direct. The Soviet Union and its satellites in Europe and elsewhere existed in a state of tension with the USA and its allies. This 'Cold War' was not over until 1991 when the USSR collapsed due to primarily economic factors as Communism was unable to beat free market capitalism. One facet of this struggle was espionage, as each side tried to steal military secrets off the other and so gain a lead over the other.

One chapter in this war of spies was played out in Ruislip. Peter and Helen Kroger had lived in a bungalow in Cranley Drive, Ruislip, since 1955, and seemed to be a respectable middle-aged, middle-class couple. They were Americans. Kroger travelled into London each day to run an antiquarian book shop in the Strand, whilst his wife stayed at home. He was well-known and liked in professional circles and his wife was sociable with their neighbours. Nothing could be more conventional.

On Sunday afternoon 8 January 1961, Detective Superintendent George Smith of the Special Branch, along with Chief Inspector Smith and other officers, went to the Krogers' house and knocked on the door. Kroger answered and Smith explained who he was. Superintendent Smith recalled:

He invited me into the lounge with the chief inspector and I said, 'I would like to see your wife as well'. A few moments later, Mrs Kroger came in and I said to them both, 'I am Superintendent Smith of the Special Branch. I would like you to tell me the name and address of the gentleman who comes and stays with you each weekend, particularly the first Saturday in every month. He arrives at about 7.15 pm.'

Mrs Kroger looked at her husband and neither made any reply. I said, 'Would you care to tell me?' Mr Kroger replied, 'Well, we have lots of friends.' I said, 'Will you name them – those who stayed with you at weekends?'

They both mentioned a number of names but no addresses. They made no reference to Lonsdale [a Soviet agent]. I then said, 'I am arresting you and shall take you to a police station and detain you. I have a warrant here to search the house.'

Mrs Kroger then went to the bedroom to get ready for leaving. She took an overcoat from the wardrobe and picked up her handbag. She said to the police, 'As I am going out for some time, may I go and stoke the boiler?' The request was agreed to, provided that she show them the contents of her handbag. She then gripped it tightly, but it was taken from her. Inside was a white envelope. After this Mrs Kroger significantly evinced no interest in stoking the boiler.

The envelope contained a six-page letter written in Russian and a single page of a block of typed numbers, which might be a code or cipher. Finally there was a typed sheet with lists of addresses and map references, probably a record of meeting places. In the handbag was a piece of glass with microdots on it. These dots were tiny pieces of film. They were used to represent a large amount of information, which could be enlarged so it became readable if the correct equipment was used. It was a method of concealing a large amount of information so that it could be transferred secretly. A bookseller, sending a book overseas, could easily include a microdot in the book. Excellent cover for spies.

Earlier that day Henry Houghton and Ethel Gee, civil servants working for the Admiralty at the Portland Naval Base, had met Gordon Lonsdale, allegedly a company director, in London in order to hand over a certain package. They had been arrested and on the following day all five appeared at Bow Street Magistrates' Court to be charged with breaking

Cranley Drive, Ruislip, 2007. Author's collection

the Official Secrets Act of 1911 between June 1960 and January 1961. They were all detained in custody, despite applications on their parts for bail. Kroger said he needed bail because he had a business to look after and so he needed to take steps to ensure its continued smooth running and he needed his wife's help in this, as well as in running their home. Their lawyer said they 'were people of perfectly good character' and, in any case, the police had confiscated their passports.

Meanwhile the police made a thorough search of the Krogers' house. Although the exterior seemed just like many other suburban dwellings, the interior boasted rather different features. First of all, the security features were extensive, being described in court thus, 'On the front door there were two locks, a chain and bolts. There were bolts and two locks on the kitchen door, and there were locking devices on all the windows, as well as the normal catches.'

There were also a number of items hidden in the house, including a number of espionage devices. In the bedroom was a microscope, capable of reading information found in microdots. There were New Zealand passports for both Krogers. In a Bible were cellophane papers coated with silver bromide, of the type used by the Soviet Secret Service in the manufacture of microfilm. Then there were a number of ordinary items which had secret cavities within them. A flask contained, in its cavity, iron oxide powder, which could be used for reading Morse recorded on a tape recorder. The base of a cigarette lighter contained two small black negatives, three small prints with figures and letters and six small rolls which were parts of code machines.

At the back of the house was a large radiogram and headphones for receiving messages. There was a microdot reader in a false bottom of a talcum powder container. Under the kitchen floor was a wireless transmitter, suitable for sending information to Moscow. Incoming calls after 9 January were monitored: they were coming from Russia. In the attic were large sums of American money; some $8,000 in total. However, despite all the police searches, it was not until 1977 that the house yielded its last secrets – a radio transmitter found buried in the garden.

The real names of the Krogers were Maurice and Lona Cohen. They were both Americans. Peter Kroger had been born in 1911 in the Bronx. He became a teacher and later studied at Illinois University, where he became a Communist. In 1937–8 he was a member of the International Brigade and fought with the Communists in Spain. Soon after returning to the USA he met the woman who would become his wife.

She had been born in Massachusetts in 1913 and worked as a servant, later as a governess, in New York. She, too, had far left views and probably met her future husband at a Communist rally. They married in 1941. At this time, her husband was working for a Soviet organization. He was called up to join the American army during the Second World War, but though he went abroad did not see any active service.

After the war, he returned to teaching. The couple had lost none of their political beliefs and continued to associate with like-minded people. These included Soviet agents, such as a man known as Colonel Abel. They also associated with the Rosenbergs, who stole atomic secrets from the USA. In 1950, with the FBI investigating left-wing circles, the Krogers changed their names and left the country. They spent some years in Australia and New Zealand where they were undetected.

Meanwhile the Soviet Union, in its bid to build up its submarine fleet, knew it needed to probe the West's anti-submarine secrets. A weak link had been detected in the form of Houghton, who had worked at the British Embassy in Poland and was known to have an expensive weakness for alcohol. He might exchange secrets for money and he was now working as a clerk at the Admiralty's base at Portland, which was a centre of British, American and other NATO secrets for the detection of submarines.

A Soviet agent, known as Gordon Lonsdale, entered Britain in 1955. So did the Krogers. He appeared to be a Canadian who was also a student learning Chinese and a director of a company specializing in selling vending machines. He was a highly competent spy and soon started doing business with Houghton and his girlfriend, Ethel Gee. Due to sloppy security at Portland, the two traitors were able to pass on secrets with relative ease. Lonsdale then relayed them to the Krogers who transmitted them to Moscow. Kroger's cover as a book dealer meant that he could send books overseas – which could include microdots with secret information in them.

The spy ring operated successfully for some years. But the weak link was Houghton. He spent far more money, mainly on drink, than a low-ranking civil servant could possibly earn. This was mentioned to a Special Branch man and investigated. It was confirmed. For the next few months Houghton, Gee and Lonsdale were tailed. The conclusion came on 8 January, as stated.

Sir Reginald Manning-Butler described it thus: 'The little suburban house was the communication centre of this spy ring, no doubt getting instructions from Moscow and supplying information by wireless or by the use of microdots.' The hearing took place at Marylebone Magistrates' Court on 7 February. It was revealed that Gee and Houghton had access to naval secrets, and had taken some, including Admiralty pamphlets, test pamphlets and film containing photographs of a top-secret document, 'Particulars of War Vessels'. All of these would be of value to the Soviet Union, since they included details of ships and submarines, and fleet orders. Since early July 1960; a watch had been kept on the two. On a number of occasions they had been seen arriving in London and meeting Lonsdale, passing on packages to him. They usually met on the first Saturday of each month, especially in October and November.

The next port of call was Ruislip. On 24 October Lonsdale had been seen taking a package to Ruislip Manor station. At first it was not found where he went after that, but Cranley Drive was not far away. On the evening of 5 November, his car was seen parked at Willow Gardens, not far from Cranley Drive. It remained there until the following morning. On that morning Mrs Kroger left the house and parked the car in front of their house. Lonsdale went to his car. Ten minutes later Mrs Kroger returned to the house. Lonsdale then reappeared and went into the house too. As the tail, 'Mr I' reported, 'He was behaving furtively and looking back from whence he had come … He went into the house very quickly through the front door. He did not appear to use a key.' 'Miss K' saw Lonsdale being driven to the house by the Krogers on 11 December.

Some of this surveillance had taken place from the house of Bill and Ruth Search, which overlooked the Krogers'. On 5 November Jim Skardon of MI5 had announced that their house would be used for surveillance purposes for two weeks (which turned out to be two months). This was much to the distress of the family there, who were on good terms with the Krogers. The latter had presented the Searches with silver coffee spoons for their twenty-fifth wedding anniversary. It was especially difficult for Mrs Search, for she had to live twenty-four hours a day with the MI5 girls, whereas at least her husband was out at work for much of the time. Her daughter later said that her mother never went to sleep without thinking how the Krogers were, and her husband later wondered if it shortened her life. They had to keep quiet and say nothing to their erstwhile friends. They found the truth about them hard to believe. The Krogers had been a generous and respectable couple. No one could have believed that they were dedicated Communists and professional spies. However, from the point of view of the security services, the operation was a success.

Ruislip Manor tube station, 2007.
Author's collection

At the trial the defence suggested that the reason for all the security on the house was that the value of the antiquarian books within made it imperative that they be there. Mrs Kroger said that Lonsdale was merely a friend who did odd jobs for them. It was also said that Lonsdale had planted the material on the unsuspecting couple. This was not very convincing.

The Krogers were found guilty and sentenced to twenty years imprisonment. Mrs Kroger was sent to Holloway and her husband to Parkhurst on the Isle of Wight. A psychological analysis showed that he had had assertive, antagonistic parents, whom he disliked. He had had a bad education, and had absurd literary pretensions. Whilst in prison, it was noted that he had not missed his wife.

However the Krogers were not to serve their full term in prison. In June 1969; negotiations between the British and Soviet governments were concluded over the possibility of an exchange. One Gerald Brooke, a London lecturer, had been arrested in the Soviet Union for allegedly distributing anti-Soviet literature, and was sentenced to five years imprisonment. Concerns over his health led, in October, to an exchange. On 20 October Kroger was transferred from Parkhurst to Brixton and, four days later, he and his wife were flown to Warsaw and returned to the Soviet Union in 1972. This caused some political controversy, with the Foreign Secretary being attacked by the opposition for allowing two dangerous spies to go free and setting a precedent whereby any British businessman or tourist in the Soviet bloc could be arrested and then used as a pawn in negotiations. Mrs Kroger died in 1993.

The case was made by British Lions as a film, *Ring of Spies*, starring Margaret Tyzack, Bernard Lee (a year before he began to play M in the James Bond films) and David Kossoff as Kroger. It could not be shown until 1970. There was also a play, *Pack of Lies*, written by Hugh Whitemore, which ran at the West End in 1983. It focused on the personal relationships and dilemmas of the Searches, played by Michael Williams and Judi Dench.

Although the unmasking of the spy ring had been presented as a triumph of British counter-espionage, it had not been a wholly unsuccessful affair for the Soviet Union either. Many secrets had been forwarded from Britain to the USSR over at least five years. Security loopholes had been discovered and new procedures were urgently needed.

CHAPTER 22

Manslaughter, Murder and Suicide, 1962

I did not mean to harm the girl. I don't know what
came over me.

E dward Donald Garlick, born in 1937, had a difficult life and had experience of the three different forms of sudden death mentioned in this chapter's title. Dr Lindesay, consultant psychiatrist at St Ebba's Hospital in Epsom, noted in 1958 that 'He feared his father, somewhat as a child as the father had a violent temper and used to go for his mother.' His parents had 'looked upon him as a weakly individual of general inadequate type'. At school Garlick was a poor mixer, did not play games and never got on with his peers, who teased him. He was not very clever either, being described as 'slightly retarded'.

He was living in Epsom in 1960 and it was here that he met one Barbara, mother to two illegitimate children and nearly ten years his senior. On 28 March 1961 he married her. They then moved from Epsom and initially lived in a caravan in Henley. Despite leaving a peripatetic lifestyle and having two children together, Dr Brisby, medical officer at Brixton prison, wrote: 'he assures me they have been quite happy. The wife also says that their life has been perfectly happy.' This was despite Garlick's flitting in and out of a number of jobs, such was his bad timekeeping. By 1962, the Garlicks were living in rented accommodation in Prince's Park Lane, Hayes, and he was employed as a storeman. But violent death and Garlick were not to be apart for long.

On Thursday 11 October 1962 Garlick was running after his landlord's dog, an eighteen-month-old black and brown mongrel called Curley, whilst on a walk with his wife and their

Prince's Park Lane, Hayes, 2007. Author's collection

two small children. He was ill and so had been signed off work for a few days. They were walking to Harmondsworth to see Mrs Ford, an aunt, who they saw occasionally. Apparently Garlick tripped over a girl's corpse whilst chasing the dog across a field off Cherry Lane, West Drayton. He later recalled:

> I saw her body and then got up and ran. I was absolutely stunned and it took me some time to come to my senses. I ran across a road to ask a workman if I could use his telephone. He thought I was joking when I said I had found a body. Eventually I managed to talk him into letting me use the phone, but I was so shocked I dialled the wrong number a couple of times. When I did dial 999 I could not get through so I had to leave it and went to stop a passing motorist.

Garlick waved his handkerchief and finally stopped a passing motorist. Frank Squire of Richings Park, Buckinghamshire, recalled: 'I was in two minds about stopping.' Garlick told him: 'Get the police there's a woman dead behind this hedge.' Squires did not entirely believe him, so went to look for himself. He saw the girl's body. The clothing and hair were still neatly arranged, but there was blood all over the front of her dress. Her purse lay at her feet and the strap of her handbag was hooked over her left foot. Squire told the police: 'It made me fell pretty sick seeing the body. I regard myself as a normal sort of man.' Garlick was also affected; he later said he felt sick on seeing the body and was unable to speak of his discovery to his wife. He added 'the dog had got him into trouble'.

The police arrived and noted that the corpse had been gagged and had been stabbed to death. They sealed off the area and erected screens where the body was found. Only residents were allowed into Cherry Lane itself. Philip Sherwood, local historian, recalled driving from Uxbridge towards Harlington on that day, and being unable to drive down Cherry Lane. Searches for physical clues were made in the locality, especially in fields and ditches. Seven metal detectors were employed. House-to-house calls were also made in an effort to find witnesses. It was noted that, a few years earlier, at Cranford Park, about a mile from the place where this body had been found, there had been the unsolved murder of Mrs Muriel Maitland.

Later that day, James White, a crane driver, and father of two, who lived in a council house on East Road, West Drayton, went to Uxbridge Mortuary and identified the body as that of Carol Ann White, his second daughter. Sixteen-year-old Carol Ann had gone missing from her parents' house on the evening of Wednesday 10 October 1962. She had gone to a telephone kiosk for 9 in the evening, where her 23-year-old fiancé, Peter Watson, who lived in Guildford, had promised to ring her, in order to arrange a date for the following evening. They had been telephoning like this for the past three weeks and he went round to see her in his bubble car on weekends. The two had met at a party in the previous year at Uxbridge, where Peter had been stationed during part of his National Service in the RAF. Carol had left home at 8.50 and then returned twenty minutes later, as her usual telephone box was engaged and she needed her purse. She then went out again. She could not get through, so rang one of Peter's neighbours, who went out to find him. The two never spoke on this occasion or on any other afterwards. And Carol was never seen alive again, except by her killer.

East Road, West Drayton, 2007. Author's collection

Shortly after 10 o'clock, James White began to become anxious about his daughter. Arriving at the telephone box, he found her pink plastic purse (which contained 6s 9d) and a pencil he had lent her. He then conducted a one-man search for her in the dark, giving up at midnight and only then contacting the police. This cannot have been a very extensive search as her corpse was only 300 yards from the telephone box.

A post-mortem examination revealed that the girl had died from internal haemorrhage caused by seven stab wounds to her chest sometime before midnight on 10 October. Five wounds had penetrated her lungs. The weapon was thought to be a six-inch stiletto type of dagger. There was also a piece of cloth in her mouth, 'so firmly pushed in that she could not have pushed it in herself'. The police thought that her killer watched her make the telephone call and then attacked her. They were anxious to trace a black Vauxhall car, which had been seen with its lights on, parked near to a telephone box on Cherry Lane on the night of the murder. Cars driving along Cherry Lane were stopped and motorists questioned.

A number of people came forward to tell the police about Carol's personality. A former school acquaintance, John

Stevens said, 'Carol did not go about with boys at school a lot, but there was one, I cannot remember his name, who did … I have never seen Carol hanging about the street or with boys that did not come to her home.' He recalled seeing Carol and Peter going to church together. Her father said that Peter was the only boyfriend and he had been introduced to the rest of the family. According to him, 'Carol was not the sort of young woman to go out with any man. So far as I know she was very fond of Peter Watson her boyfriend.' Colin Covacic said, 'Carol was a very nice girl, she was fairly quiet and she liked the company of boys.'

Detective Inspector Field made the following initial statement to the press:

> We are still of the opinion that the youth was known to the girl and it does appear from witnesses that this man and the dead girl walked down Cherry Lane together, she going voluntarily into the field. We still think that at 9.30 pm there must have been some people about Cherry Lane who have seen something, but have not come forward.

One hundred officers were involved in the case and thousands of people were interviewed. Every house on the Bell council estate was called on. One witness said that someone matching Carol's description was seen near the Cherry Tree pub, on the corner of Cherry Lane and Sipson Road.

Two weeks later the police were wanting to find a youth who had the words 'Love and Hate' tattooed on his hands. He was thought to possess an old blue van and was working at Stockley fair on the previous week, a fair that Carol was thought to have attended. Several people contacted the police with information about men they knew who matched this description. The most important was the testimony of three lads who had been cycling down Cherry Lane at 9.15 on the night of the murder. Yet their testimony was uncertain. Christopher Denny, a schoolboy, told them:

> I saw two people coming towards us on the right hand side from the direction of Sipson Road. I couldn't tell if they

The Fox and Pheasant, formerly the Cherry Tree, 2007. Author's collection

were men or women; it was too dark. They crossed the road and went to the field through the opening...These people were roughly the same height. They were walking very close together.

Another witness said, 'I know Carol White only very vaguely and because of the darkness and the short time which I looked in her direction, I cannot say whether the girl I saw in the field was Carol White or not.' He did not see a parked car nearby.

Exhaustive enquiries were made. Men at the West Drayton RAF base were questioned and cleared. It was said that Superintendent Osborne was putting pressure on his men to solve this most violent murder.

Yet the killer was already known to the police – and had been right from the start, had they but known it. It was three weeks before an arrest was made. On the evening of 29 October Garlick was questioned again about the murder. The police had become increasingly suspicious about his story about finding the body. They wanted to know about his movements on the night of the murder. That he was absent from home that night was undoubted. One Daisy Hellewell had visited at 8.30 and stayed until 10.10, and Garlick had been away from home all that time.

Garlick could explain all that. He told the police that he had been ill with migraine and sinus trouble, and had been signed off work by his doctor. So on the Wednesday evening, he went out in search of aspirin tablets. He called at a number of pubs. The Pear Tree did not stock what he wanted, nor did the Hut pub, but he bought cigarettes from the latter. He then walked to the Crown in Colham Green and was again unlucky. He sat outside the pub and smoked. He tried a pub near Hillingdon Hospital next. After that he went home, being unable to buy the pills anyway. He cut his hand clambering over the back fence on his way home. When he was questioned about owning a knife, he replied that he had had one and had given it to his stepson, Stephen, but that it had later been thrown out. When he bought another, which he had in his possession at the time of the murder, he put it on the roof of the garden shed. Summarizing, he said:

> I did not go into Cherry Lane on that Wednesday night. I am sure it was not me who attacked the girl on Cherry Lane and I am quite prepared for the police to examine all my clothing and to take a sample of my blood to prove my innocence.

He then refused to sign the statement, saying 'If I sign it and you find blood on my clothes, you and everyone will say that I am a liar.'

Garlick's account was not corroborated with anyone else. Publicans were interviewed and none recalled seeing him on the night in question. Alice Nethecott, who ran the Pear Tree, said, 'I have spoken to all my staff who were on duty that evening. Those who know Garlick have no knowledge of his calling.'

Field questioned Garlick again, on the following day. This time he gave a different account of the evening. According to Garlick, he had been out that night looking for pills, and walked down Falling Lane, along Yiewsley High Street, and under the railway bridge, reaching Sipson Road. He saw Carol by a telephone kiosk in Cherry Lane. Garlick claimed to have

Cherry Lane, West Drayton, 2007. Author's collection

met her previously. He said, 'I knew her, I had met her about seven months ago when I had a car. I had met her then in Yiewsley by a bus stop and offered a lift. That time I took her in my car to the estate at West Drayton.' He introduced himself as a married man, 'after that first time I met her we arranged to meet that weekend to go to the pictures. I was to see her at the bus station at Yiewsley, but I didn't show up.'

On the fatal 10th, Garlick stated: 'She was standing by the box in Cherry Lane. We chatted and I asked her for a light for my fag. I did not get a light. I said what about coming for a walk.' Carol said she knew a place where no one would see them. They then went into the field through the gap in the hedge as described by the lads. Then, according to Garlick, 'We laid down on the grass, I was on her left side. We started kissing, she didn't mind, she liked it. Then she took her knickers off.' They had sex twice (on the second occasion, she insisted Garlick put a rag into her mouth so she would not scream out), and, afterwards:

'She put her clothes straight and took the rag out of her mouth and started talking about she would have to go. Then I went mad. She was lying down. I am on her left. I got my knife in my left hand and pushed it into her... . I forgot to tell you about this knife. I had it in my inside blazer pocket and as we walked down Cherry Lane I showed it to her. I didn't threaten her with it. I offered it to her. She took it and put it in her handbag. She didn't seem to be nervous. She didn't show it. When she was straightening herself up, she took her handbag and she gave me the knife back. That was when I went mad and put it in her. I do not know how many times I stabbed her.

Garlick claimed that Carol had taunted him about his performance and that this was the cause of his killing her. We do not know for certain how truthful this statement was. It certainly suggests that Carol was promiscuous and happy to cheat on her boyfriend, even though she was waiting to speak to him – distance scarcely making the heart fonder. These go against the statements made about her by others earlier in the investigation, though people rarely speak ill of those recently murdered. And the evidence of the boys suggests that the two went into the field amicably enough and Carol was willing to go with Garlick. If Garlick was correct, then she was clearly unaware what danger she was in and made fun of him, which proved fatal for her.

He spent about fifteen to twenty minutes in the field, before returning home. He said, 'The next day all this seemed a nightmare to me.' Asked why he decided to 'find' the body on the next day, he said, 'I went in just to see if it was all true.' Finally, he tried to excuse his actions, 'I have had a lot of worry, my wife has not been well and we are living with two kids in one room, I have had migraine a lot recently, the doctor reckons its worry that caused it. I did not mean to harm the girl. I don't know what came over me.'

After first saying that the knife was on the roof of his shed, Garlick then took the police to his back garden and, buried under three inches of soil near a post, he found the knife. He then asked 'Can I see my wife; perhaps she will remember where the knife is.' On meeting, the two embraced and she asked him, 'Did you do it?' The answer was short: 'Yes. I did it.' Garlick told her he was going to confess, but she was adamant that he did not do it. Eventually, his wife, Barbara, aged 32, said, 'I will wait for you forever.'

Meanwhile investigations had gone on into Garlick's past. He was known to the police and his former years had been well documented. He had initially lived in Cranford, marrying Wendy June at St Dunstan's in 1957 and in the following year the two lived in rented rooms in the top storey of a house in Mosslea Road, Penge. The two seemed happy, as their landlady recalled, 'During the time they were in my house, Mr and Mrs Garlick were a very quiet couple and very much in love.' Garlick had drifted in and out of work ever since he had left school and at this time was a machine operator. The two were unable to manage their financial affairs and were in debt, to the tune of £9 5s 3d. Garlick recalled: 'We were hopelessly in debt when we arrived at Mosslea Road'. Desperate times seem to suggest desperate measures. Garlick said: 'Wendy suggested she went to Piccadilly for a few weeks to go with men and get some money. She went for two nights.'

Worse was to follow. Garlick suggested: 'I said to her "I'm fed up with this, what about committing suicide?" I was fed up thinking about all the bills and Wendy turned round and said she didn't feel like living.' However, it was uncertain how far his wife agreed to the suicide pact, for she replied, 'If you want to do it, you do it.' On the morning of 28 September 1958, Garlick and his wife were in a sealed room and he turned on the gas taps. She tried to turn them off, there was a struggle and she fell and hit her head. According to Garlick, he then tried to turn the taps off.

When the two were later found, a knife lay across Mrs Garlick's corpse. Dr Dennis Kelleher said, 'I thought he was suffering from the effects of coal and gas … She was dead.' Brian Culliford, senior scientific officer at Scotland Yard, discovered that the level of carbon monoxide in her body was 38 per cent and said this level of 'saturation is within the range of lethal concentration of carbon monoxide'.

Garlick was taken to Beckenham Hospital. He could not be questioned by the police immediately for, as a doctor advised, 'Any person who has had his brain deprived of oxygen is liable to have his memory affected … I would say any statement made by a person who has been unconscious from carbon monoxide poisoning must be carefully scrutinised.'

Although Garlick was charged with murdering his wife, psychiatric reports were made. Dr Lindesay noted 'the patient has also been on night work and tended to get very depressed, worrying about his debts and describing himself as always being of a worrying disposition'. However, he was not insane. There was

> No history of past mental illness ... no delusions or hallucinations, no evidence of psychosis ... nor did I have the impression that the patient was schizophrenic. I think it could be reasonably argued that the depression had reached a pitch in which he could be said to have suffered from a degree of abnormality of mind which would substantially reduce his responsibility at the time the offence occurred.

James Brown, senior medical officer, at Canterbury prison observed:

> Garlick isn't a good informant and my embarrassing questions tend to meet with the answer 'I can't remember'. I have been unable to elicit evidence of mental disorder. He displays no signs of remorse or particular emotion in describing his wife's life or death. In my opinion he is not insane.

The question of sanity was important, for if Garlick was insane he clearly could not be held responsible in law for his actions and so might be sent to Broadmoor. He was sane enough to stand trial, though for manslaughter, not murder, on 24 November 1958. He was given a lenient sentence – three years to be spent in Epsom, where he had to 'be of good behaviour and lead an industrious life', as well as reporting regularly to the probation service. He was being given a second chance – a fine liberal gesture to this young man.

So Garlick had killed before. Returning to 1962, after his arrest he appeared before Uxbridge Magistrates' Court. He was remanded in custody until 8 November. Detective Superintendent Maurice Osborne said to him, 'You have already admitted murdering Carol White on October 10 and you are now going to be formally charged.' Once again Garlick was examined by doctors. Although he was viewed as dim-witted, he was not insane. Sir Paul Malleson wrote, 'his answers were fluent and rather convincing'. He was aware of his surroundings and was fit to plead.

The trial took place at the Old Bailey on 29 January 1963 and lasted three days, partly because it had to be adjourned on the first day due to a juror falling ill. Garlick pleaded 'not guilty'. The prosecution had no doubt that Carol had been 'the victim of a brutal and callous murder', but that no motive could be ascertained. The defence claimed that the police had 'fastened on' Garlick because discoveries had been made about his past and because the detectives were being pressurized to pull in someone for the murder. Field said this was untrue: 'No sir, suspicion fell on him when we did not get truthful answers to the questions.' The prosecutor claimed:

Can you see anybody, simply because they have been detained at a police station for a few hours confessing to this crime if he had nothing to do with it at all? Can you really accept that if he was threatened, and if threatened that he believed the police would bring in not only his wife as an accessory, but his stepson, aged 11, who didn't even live in the same house? Or is it all a fairy story?

Dr Francis Brisby, principal medical office at Brixton prison, where Garlick had been held prior to the trial, said that although the accused was slightly below average intelligence, he was not mentally defective.

Eventually, after considering their verdict for an hour and twenty minutes, the jury found Garlick to be guilty. Garlick then alleged that he had only signed the confession because the police had threatened to accuse his wife and 11-year-old stepson with being accessories after the fact. Although Garlick was convinced that he would only receive a year's sentence in a mental hospital, he was sentenced to life imprisonment. He made no comment at the sentence. Perhaps he was lucky to escape execution.

In 1981 he was in Leyhill open prison in Gloucestershire, a liberal ruling for such a violent criminal. On a weekend in August, he went to see his parents in Ramsgate for the weekend and never returned. On 24 August Wiltshire police found a decapitated body of a man in a tunnel on the railway line near Chippenham. It was that of Garlick. A fitting end. There was no suspicion of foul play. Unlike the case in 1958, he had been successful in his attempt to commit suicide. Why he chose this time to do so is unknown. Did he feel remorse? If so, it seems odd that he did so, almost two decades after killing Carol White.

Conclusion

I t is now time to draw some conclusions from this examination of murders in and around Uxbridge. Of the sixteen cases where murder definitely occurred, all the killers but one were male. Each only killed one victim, except for Owen (seven), Williams (three) and Garlick (two). Of these twenty-four victims, six were men, eight were children and ten were women. Five killers used knives or daggers, in eleven cases bludgeons were used, three were killed by gas, two were strangled, one was shot and another was killed by a chopper. One was drowned. Money was the uppermost motive with two killers, revenge for another two, three killed because of verbal provocation, insanity and drunkenness each led one killer to kill, the desire to conceal his identity lead to another murder, and one died due to a double suicide. Five motives are unknown. As to the ultimate fate of the killers: six were sent to prison, two were executed, one was transported, one committed suicide, one was acquitted and four were undetected. One may have been sent to Bedlam. A third of the murderers whose deeds chronicled here escaped punishment. These crimes took place throughout what is now the modern borough of Hillingdon, with two each in Harefield, Hayes, Uxbridge and West Drayton, three in Ruislip and Yiewsley and one in Northwood.

Yet there were long periods of time when no murders were committed – none being recorded between 1816 and 1837, 1839 and 1869 and 1906 and 1934 for instance. Since the 1930s, no decade had been free of murder, though this may be in part due to an increased population. Even so, to have four murders in the 1930s, five in the 1940s and six in the 1950s (on average less than one per year) is hardly an epidemic by modern standards. Recent figures for 2005–7 record ten, which is a low number among London boroughs but far more than in the past (it exceeds the total number of murders committed in the 1930s and 1940s). This may be due to changes in society and the abolition of the death penalty.

Bibliography

PRIMARY SOURCES

Manuscript
The National Archives: Metropolitan Police, MEP20/1–5 Murder and Manslaughter Files; MEP02/1723, MEP03/1735; CRIM1/731, 964, 1735, 4070; HO64/7; Will of William Howard
Uxbridge Library: 'Crime file: depositions relating to the murder of Mr Howard, 1816–1817'
Principal Registry of the Family Division: Will of James Gibbons

Printed
The Annual Register, 1816.
Buckinghamshire Advertiser, 1869
Calendar of State Papers Domestic, Henry VIII, 1530–1534.
Morning Courier, 1816
The Times, 1839, 1869, 1870, 1884, 1938, 1954, 1961, 1962–3
Southall-Norwood Gazette, 1895, 1899, 1906
Middlesex County Times, 1895, 1934
Middlesex Advertiser and Gazette, 1884, 1895, 1899, 1906, 1954, 1962, 1963
The Illustrated Police News, 1895, 1937
Sunday Telegraph, 1983
Foxe's Martyrs
G Hutson, *Recollections of Uxbridge* (1985)

Kelly's Directories for Middlesex
Middlesex County Records: Sessions Rolls, vol, 1 (1886)
C Harper, *Rural Nooks around London* (1907)
J Bulloch and H Miller, *Spy Ring* (1961)
Census Returns, 1851–1901
M S Briggs, *Middlesex, Old and New* (1934)
St John's Hillingdon, Parish register transcripts

Electronic
Oldbaileyonline

SECONDARY SOURCES
Oxford Dictionary of National Biography
E Bowlt, *Ruislip Past* (1994)
C Cotton, *Uxbridge Past* (1994)
A H Cox, *West Drayton and Yiewsley through the Centuries* (1983)
G R Elton, *Star Chamber Stories* (1958)
Furneaux, *Criminal Cases*, vol. 2 (1954)
A Neames, *Elizabeth Barton* (1971)
P Read, 'Denham Murder Postscript', *Hilliingdon Family History Society Journal*, 77 (2007)
Victoria County History for Middlesex, vols 3 and 4

Index

Alsop, Joseph   55–62, 64
Barton, Elizabeth   30–2
Bond, John   41–6
Bond, Thomas   41, 45–6
Bonner, Bishop   34–5
Bray, James   47, 49–51, 54
Brentford   33, 80, 93, 113
Brill, John   7, 47–9, 52–3
Buckingham   114, 116,
   118
Butler, Charles   107, 109
Clayton, Thomas   104,
   123, 129
Chamberlain, Lilian
   144–7, 149–51
Christie, Reginald   25, 162
Cliff, Alfred   124–6, 129
Cliff, William   124–9
Coker, George   65–8
Cranmer, Archbishop   31,
   33
Davidson, John   135–42
Davidson, Olive   135–6,
   139–42
Davidson, Thomas   135,
   137–43
Denley, John   33–6
Dicconson, Harry   110
Ealing   101–3, 106, 110,
   136, 138, 160, 165–6
Ferris, Dr John   72–5,
   85–7, 112
Garlick, Edmund   177–9,
   182–90
Gates, Moses   65–6
Gibbons, Elizabeth
   93–100
Gibbons, James   93–100
Gold, Revd Henry   10,
   27–32

Gold, Thomas   28–32
Grand Junction canal   12,
   43, 101, 104–5, 111, 113,
   119, 122, 126, 137–8,
   140–1
Greenford   113, 116,
   166
Grierson, Dr Hugh   141,
   149
Hammond, William   106,
   109
Hanwell   88, 113, 135
Hayden, Dr William   105,
   107–8, 123–5
Henry VIII   31–3
Higgs, Sarah   12, 101–10,
   123
High Wycombe   113, 118–19
Howard, William   41,
   43–4, 46, 54
Hutson, Giles   11, 20–1,
   24, 26
Kemp, Reginald   123, 129,
   131, 134
Kroger, Helen   7, 169–176
Kroger, Peter   7, 169–176
Lamb, Charles   49–54
Lavender, Thomas   47,
   49–51, 54
Maidenhead   114
Maidstone   33
Marshall family   77–80,
   84–90
Mary, Queen   33, 36
Medhurst, Francis   55–64,
   67–8
Murray, William   7, 24,
   69–76
Owen, John   80–4, 87–92,
   190

Packingham, Patrick   34–6
Paul, Claire   152–9
Paul, Sidney   152–9
Perryman, William
   111–12, 119–21
Potter, Frank.   103, 109
Randall, Sarah   41–2, 44
Reading   81–3, 89
Redrup, Frederick   69–73,
   75–6, 85
Rickmansworth   47,
   146–7
Rodgers, John   145–51
Rose, Norman   140–2
Slough   83, 114
Smith, Robert   35–6
Southall   102, 140
Spilsbury, Sir Bernard
   138, 145, 154, 157
Stevenson, Sir Thomas
   134
Story, Dr   35–6
Sturmer, Revd Frederick
   12, 55–9, 61, 63–4
Tilbury, Charles   112–22
Tilbury, Rosetta   112–22
Townsend, Jean   18,
   160–7
Trumper, Edward   37–40
Walker, Ann   37–40
Walker, William   37–40
White, Carol   23, 179–85,
   188–9
Williams, Anne   131–4
Williams, Edward
   Montague   131–4, 190
Wiseman, Sir William   46,
   52